Also by James Haskins with Kathleen Benson:
  Scott Joplin: The Man Who Made Ragtime

Also by James Haskins:
  The Cotton Club
  Bricktop (with Bricktop)
  Adam Clayton Powell: Portrait of a Marching Black
  I'm Gonna Make You Love Me: The Story of Diana Ross
  Donna Summer
  James Van DerZee: The Picture Takin' Man
  Katherine Dunham
  Black Theater in America
  Voodoo & Hoodoo
  Diary of a Harlem Schoolteacher
  Barbara Jordan
  The Life and Death of Martin Luther King, Jr.

Also by Kathleen Benson:
  A Man Called Martin Luther

LENA

A Personal and Professional Biography of Lena Horne

James Haskins
with Kathleen Benson

STEIN AND DAY/*Publishers*/New York

First published in 1984
Copyright © 1984 by James Haskins and Kathleen Benson
All rights reserved, Stein and Day, Incorporated
Designed by Terese B. Platten
Printed in the United States of America
STEIN AND DAY/*Publishers*
Scarborough House
Briarcliff Manor, NY 10510

Library of Congress Cataloging in Publication Data

Haskins, James, 1941-
  Lena: a personal and professional biography of
Lena Horne.

  Includes index.
  1. Horne, Lena.   2. Singers—United States—Biography.
I. Benson, Kathleen.   II. Title.
ML420.H65H38   1984   784.5'0092'4   [B]   81-48456
ISBN 0-8128-2853-4

ACKNOWLEDGMENTS

The authors wish to thank Joan "Halimah" Brooks, Dalili Davis, Ann L. Kalkhoff, and Frances Williams for their help.

CONTENTS

ILLUSTRATIONS

Lena at age sixteen
In 1934, when Lena was a chorus girl at the Cotton Club
Avon Long and Lena, 1934
With Noble Sissle, 1936
Lena, ca. 1935-1940
Thornton Hall and Lena, 1943
At the Savoy-Plaza, New York, 1943
With Paul Robeson, 1947
Lena in *Broadway Rhythm*, 1944
At the London Casino, 1947
Lena in Paris, 1950
Arriving in New York with Lennie, 1950
With Lennie in Paris, 1954
Lena in *Meet Me in Las Vegas*, 1956
At the Coconut Grove, 1956
With her daughter, Gail, in the late 1950s
Lena in *Jamaica*, 1958-1959
With Eleanor Roosevelt in 1960
At the March on Washington, 1963
In London, 1966
On the set of *Death of a Gunfighter*, 1968
With her son-in-law, Sidney Lumet, 1971
Lena in 1975
After her 62nd birthday, 1979
With James Mason, 1982
At the Broadway opening night of *Lena Horne: The Lady and Her Music, 1981*
With a poster advertising her one-woman show in Hollywood, 1982

1

BROOKLYN-BORN
AND PROUD OF IT

THE cartoonist Virgil Partch once drew a picture of a drunk dancing on a nightclub table and shouting, "Hey, Lena Baby, sing something dirty." In the 1960s, Lena Horne captioned the cartoon "The story of my life," and it remains symbolic of most of her fifty years as an entertainer. In the Cotton Club days, when she was still jailbait, she performed in a G-string and pasties before a whites-only audience. In Hollywood, she was billed as a sepia Hedy Lamarr. In nightclubs, she was famous for giving a naughty twist to the lyrics of old favorites like "Honeysuckle Rose" and "Body and Soul." When she turned fifty she decided to "git trashy," and fifteen years later she was the sexiest senior citizen Broadway had ever seen.

Her father was a "numbers" banker. Her best friends were jazz musicians. She was Joe Louis's girl friend when he was heavyweight champion of the world. She tried never to wear the same evening gown twice. In a time when a beautiful, light-complexioned Negro girl was automatically stereotyped as a flashy whore, Lena was copper-colored and gorgeous. And what's more, she enjoyed entrée into areas of American public society from which most blacks had always been actively barred. She represented what black people both enviously and disapprovingly called the "sporting life."

That this image never did reflect the real Lena is a fact that she accepted—not entirely in protest—for most of her life. She functioned as two Lenas—the public persona and the private person—and she began to practice the required compartmentalization of her being when she was a child.

Lena Horne was born in a Brooklyn, New York, hospital on June 30, 1917. Her mother, Edna Scottron Horne, was accompanied to the hospital not by her husband, Teddy Horne, but by her mother-in-law, Cora Calhoun Horne. Teddy Horne was caught up in a card game in which he was winning the money to pay the hospital bill. Even if he had taken his wife to the hospital, his mother probably would have gone along anyway; she was a domineering woman who didn't think much of her daughter-in-law's ability to handle things.

Both Edna and Cora were very light-skinned, and the hospital staff assumed they were white. Thus, when the copper-colored Lena arrived they were at first taken aback and then oddly thrilled. They exhibited her about as if she were some accident of nature.

In retrospect, Lena feels that not just her actual life but the pattern of her childhood were established on that day. Her curious copper color was to remain a curiosity. Her father was to continue to be largely removed from her day-to-day existence; and her paternal grandmother was to be the dominant force in her early life. And the fact that she was born a colored curiosity, of light-skinned parents who belonged to the black bourgeoisie, would affect not only her childhood years, but most of the years of her life.

Lena was the product of the close-knit—indeed, fiercely insular—black middle class in the Bedford-Stuyvesant section of Brooklyn, which, in contrast to the deprived ghetto it is today, was once considered prime real estate. Both her mother's and her father's families were respected in the community, although her mother's background was a bit questionable by the community's standards. Both claimed a solid tradition of hard work, ambition, class pride, and, coincidentally, female dominance.

On her mother's side, the authority figure was Amelie Louise Ashton, Lena's great-grandmother, born in Senegal, who had long black hair, spoke French, and had nothing but disdain for American Negroes, although she apparently married one. Settling in Brooklyn, she raised her daughter, Louise, to be a member in good standing of the bourgeoisie and sent her to the only black teacher-training school in the borough. When her daughter married Cyrus Scottron, a black of Portuguese heritage from Massachusetts who was the first black railway post office clerk, she was no doubt pleased, although his family was suspect. He had two female relatives who had passed for white and gone into show business, one as a concert singer and one as an actress in vaudeville. Both "passing" and show business careers were anathema to the black middle class, and it is likely that Cyrus Scottron heard many disparaging remarks about these two relatives. He remained with his wife for eleven years after their daughter, Edna, was born, then left.

Edna Scottron was raised in a female household, one dominated by her grandmother, Amelie, who babied her and shielded her from the unpleasant realities of life. Thus, Edna grew up spoiled and pliant. However, there was a streak of rebellion in her. Secretly, she harbored the dream of going into show business the way her absent father's relatives had done; and then she fell in love with Teddy Horne who, though born into the black bourgeoisie, was hardly of it.

Of the four sons born to Edwin and Cora Calhoun Horne, Teddy was the darkest-skinned and the least conformist. Even as a small child, he had an insatiable desire to be independent. He was perpetually in trouble with the truant officer. At the age of eight he managed not only to find his way to Manhattan to apply for a job as page boy at the Astor Hotel but also to land the job. He had learned at an early age that money was the key: with money he could pay others to do his homework and bribe his brothers to do his house chores. Money also enabled him to buy gifts for his mother, Cora Calhoun Horne, who found it nearly impossible to punish him when she was being thus stroked with kindness. His father, Edwin Horne, was a quiet man who deferred to his wife in matters of child rearing as well as in most other things.

Thus, when Edna Scottron and Teddy Horne fell in love, they had little in common but comparatively light skin, good looks, and membership in the same tightly knit, middle-class black community; with dominant women in the family as a corollary similarity. Edna was a pampered princess and Teddy was a bourgeois rogue. When they married, he had disdained school and opted for work, but not just any work. He had decided that he could neither make real money nor maintain his self-respect if he settled for the idea of working for "the man." He had looked at the options for "colored men" in the 1920s, seen that the pinnacle of success for such a man was a position as a Pullman porter, and declined that great opportunity. He had looked, too, at the possibility of going into an enterprise that would serve the black community, such as the hotel or funeral business. He did not find this route very exciting, but instead chose a variation on the theme of business—he became a "numbers" runner and a gambler.

When he and Edna Scottron were married, Teddy wasn't making enough money to afford a home of his own, and he and his bride moved in with his family. Immediately there were problems. Teddy had expected his bride to grace his world with her beauty but otherwise not to bother him very much, and Edna had expected to have her own house to rule. She had not anticipated her mother-in-law's domination. Lena's birth assuaged the problems for a time, but soon the resentments began to build up again. When Lena was two, her great-grandmother, Amelie Louise Ashton, died, and Lena's mother lost her strongest supporter in her fight to maintain her integrity in the household of her husband's family. After that, the problems grew worse, and when Lena was three her father went away, leaving his wife unhappily in the home of her in-laws.

The house was a four-story brownstone on Chauncey Street,

between Reid and Patchen Avenues; by the time her father left, Lena had developed a fascination with the black wrought-iron fence with arrow-shaped spikes that separated its property from that of the neighbors. Although it was supposed to be a fence that kept other people out, Lena could not help feeling that it also kept her in, for her grandmother would not allow her to play with the children on either side. The Irish neighbors were considered low class while the Scandinavian neighbors apparently worked with cars, and Lena's grandmother didn't want her to get dirty. Due to the scarcity of acceptable playmates, Lena played in her grandparents' backyard alone.

Lena's grandmother was a formidable woman, and her credentials in the Brooklyn black middle-class community were impeccable. She was a well-known, unyielding fighter for the causes of black people. She was an active member of the Urban League, the National Association for the Advancement of Colored People (NAACP), and of the women's suffrage and Ethical Culture movements. She was also a full-time social worker in Harlem. She was thoroughly prejudiced against blacks of lower social status and against whites of any social status. She had raised her four sons, including Burke who was still at home and attending school, to be ambitious, successful men, and if she had failed with Teddy she believed she could somehow make up for that failure with Teddy's daughter, Lena. She brushed aside her daughter-in-law, Edna. Early on, she had tested Edna's strength of will and found it lacking. Well before Teddy had left, she had begun to victimize Edna. After Teddy left, it was much easier for her to assert her will.

Edna hung on for a time, primarily out of concern for her daughter. But she found it more and more difficult to live under the domination of her mother-in-law. As her sense of being trapped increased, she began to turn for refuge to her dream of being an actress, as the women in her father's family had been. At length she acted on her dream. That was perhaps also an excuse to abandon her daughter and set out on her own, as her husband had done before her.

Lena was left in the care of her grandmother and grandfather and her uncle Burke, and by this time she was about five and old enough to be aware of the family dynamics. Her grandparents rarely spoke to one another, except to say "Good morning" and "Good evening." Anything more substantive was conveyed by messenger, in the form of their son Burke, who was always carrying written and verbal messages between them. Lena learned to address her grandparents separately, not together, which was not at all difficult, since they were rarely together anyway.

She spent more time with her grandfather than with her grandmother. Edwin Horne always seemed to have more time. He was a highly intelligent man who spoke six languages, had a keen interest in the arts, and was as concerned as his wife, but in a quieter way, with Negro social and economic progress. He had attended college in Indiana, where one of his brothers had become the first Negro sheriff in the state and where another brother had been killed in a dynamite explosion set by whites who resented his successful trading on the Mississippi. While in Indiana, Edwin Horne had edited two black newspapers, *The Bee* and *The Freeman*. He had taught school in Atlanta, Georgia, and in New York; and later had been an inspector in the fire department. He taught Lena to love books and music and to appreciate such black performers of the day as Bert Williams and Florence Mills.

When her grandmother was around, which was not often, Lena was grilled about her homework at the Brooklyn Ethical School, which she was attending on the Cora Calhoun Horne Scholarship; about her playmates; and about her experiences at the various meetings to which her grandmother took her. These were meetings of the organizations to which her grandmother belonged, and Lena was usually the only child there; yet her grandmother expected her to understand what went on at the meetings and to report to her about them. Lena learned to be disciplined with her grandmother and to relax with her grandfather, aware that she could be herself only when given the leave to be so.

Lena still heard from her parents occasionally. Her father had been an excellent correspondent since he left, often sending her postcards and presents from the places he visited. Once he sent her a fur coat, and Lena's idea about him was a romantic one: she dreamed that he would come to take her away one day. Once her mother left, Lena transferred much of her yearning to her mother.

Edna had joined the Lafayette Players, a well-known Negro stock company that had been founded by the actress Anita Bush. It was based in Harlem, and, although it traveled on occasion, it did not travel so extensively that Edna could not have seen her daughter more often than she did. Edna Horne suffered from a sense of responsibility for the daughter she had left behind, but she stayed away from Chauncey Street because she couldn't stand to see her mother-in-law or endure her domineering manner. She would visit her daughter furtively, leaning over the wrought-iron fence, and promising the little girl that one day they would be together. Lena longed for that to happen, but she had already learned to suspect the promises of grown-ups.

Lena remembers that she was about seven when one day she was playing in the yard behind the house on Chauncey Street and a cousin of her mother's appeared on the opposite side of the wrought-iron fence. Her mother was very sick, the cousin told her, and she must hurry to her. Putting aside her grandmother's regulation against leaving the house until someone from the family came home, Lena quickly changed her clothes and went with her cousin. Her *mother* was sick, and that was all she needed to know.

When Lena arrived at the Harlem apartment where her mother lived, she concluded that her mother wasn't really very sick. It didn't matter. She was with her mother, and, although she had no idea what her mother's life was like, she didn't care if she never saw Brooklyn again. The important thing to her was that her new home was defined not by walls but by her relationship with someone she loved.

Although Edna Horne was far from well when an opportunity came for her to go on the road, she took the job. She now had her daughter with her, and she had to earn a living for them both. Lena went with her mother to Philadelphia, where they stayed briefly, then to Miami, where they stayed longer. In Miami Lena was cared for by a strict woman who beat her whenever she did anything that the woman thought would disturb her mother. Lena learned very quickly not to disturb her mother. Unfortunately, that also meant not telling her mother about the beatings.

She also learned, during her time in the South, not to do a lot of other disturbing things. She learned not to speak with a "Northern" accent, because the Southern children she met made fun of it. She learned not to dress the way she had been accustomed to dressing, because she was regarded as different. On occasion, she was sent back to the house on Chauncey Street for a few days or even weeks, and there she had to speak and dress differently than she did in the South. Her brief visits also forced her to play yet another role, for her grandmother wanted to know what she and her mother had been doing, and Lena felt that if she related her experiences she might be betraying her mother. She wouldn't admit to her grandmother how unhappy her nomadic life, in which she was forced to adjust constantly to new people, new places, and new situations, made her. She longed for the normal routine of Chauncey Street; it now seemed an anchor of consistency amidst the unpredictable waves of circumstance in which her young life was tossed. However, if she admitted how much she missed having roots and a real home, she knew her grandmother would insist that she stay, and she doubted that her mother would be able to stand the blow.

If nothing else, these nomadic years forced Lena to grasp and implement the techniques of survival that forever eluded her mother. Each new location provided her with an introduction to another situation to which it was necessary to adjust. The adjustments weren't always hard. She remembers with fondness her stay in a small town in Ohio while her mother was on tour. She lived with a doctor's family, and the doctor's maiden sister sat with her during the long night hours when Lena forced herself to stay awake so as not to have the recurring nightmares that had begun to plague her since Miami.

In Macon, Georgia, she lived with a poverty-stricken family

whose elderly grandmother applied home remedies to her rickets-pained legs, due to malnutrition (and probably the reason why her legs did not develop well); introduced her to Southern country cooking, and told her and the several grandchildren stories from the Bible. She was genuinely loath to leave this family who were so rich in spirit, but her uncle Frank, one of her father's brothers, visited, and appalled by the circumstances in which she was living, took her with him to Fort Valley, Georgia.

Frank taught at Fort Valley State College. As he was unmarried, it was not considered proper for his niece to live with him so Lena lived in the girls' dormitory with his fiancée, a student chaperone. She enjoyed being around the older girls and hearing their talk about sophisticated subjects like fashion and dates. She was welcomed as a fellow member of the black middle class. But at the school where she was enrolled, the other children teased her because of her color and called her "yaller."

Her father came to visit her for a few months during her second year in Fort Valley, where he went to recuperate from an automobile accident. It was her first extended contact with him since he had left her and her mother, and she was overjoyed to be with him. But her time with her father was not without unhappiness. Being with his college-professor brother, whose education he had helped to pay for, caused his antipathy to formal education to resurface. He elected to display his considerable informal education by instructing Lena in mathematics with such sternness and impatience that Lena believes he created in her a mental block against mathematics that has lasted to this day. Nonetheless, Lena remembers her two years in Fort Valley as among the happiest of her childhood, and when her mother appeared to claim her again, she wanted desperately to stay. But her loyalty to her mother was too strong.

Lena's mother and a girl friend had managed to purchase a small house in Atlanta, and it was there that Lena lived next. Not long after she arrived, her mother found temporary work in another city and left her once again in the care of strangers—a couple who moved into the house in Edna's absence. The woman

19

was unduly harsh, commanding Lena to do strenuous house chores, after which she would inspect Lena's work by running white-gloved hands over furniture surfaces. If Lena had missed a spot, she received a beating. Oddly, the beatings were always reserved for either a Wednesday or a Saturday. Frightened of upsetting her mother, Lena did not report the woman's brutality. Edna Horne had to learn from neighbors what her daughter could not tell her. She sent the couple away, but could not rid herself of her feelings of guilt for subjecting her daughter to such mistreatment.

Not long afterward, Edna and her girl friend lost the house because they were unable to keep up with the mortgage payments. Thoroughly demoralized and convinced of her inability to make a home for herself and her daughter, Edna finally gave in and sent Lena back to live with her grandparents in Brooklyn.

By the time she returned to Brooklyn, the young teenager had become so withdrawn that her grandparents were worried. They sensed that she had suffered greatly during her nomadic existence and that she had erected a protective shell around herself to buttress her frail soul from further onslaughts. The quiet support of Edwin Horne helped her to emerge slowly from that shell. Cora Calhoun Horne took a more aggressive tack. She criticized her daughter-in-law unmercifully. The ever-loyal Lena sprang to her mother's defense, and in so doing was able to express feelings that she had been unable to give voice to before. Within a year she had cast off much of the protective shell, reacquainted herself with her childhood friends and made new ones, and had begun to come out of the deep depression into which she had fallen during the hard years she'd been with her mother. Unfortunately, she then suffered the shock of losing both her grandparents in the space of a few months. Cora Calhoun Horne, who had suffered for years with bronchial asthma, succumbed to an attack. Her husband died a few months later, and Lena realized that, although theirs had not been a loving relationship, they had shared a deep dependence and that Edwin Horne had little reason to live without his wife.

Lena stayed on for a while with her uncle Burke, but he was in college and incapable of taking the responsibility for a teenager and so she went to live with a family friend, Laura Rollock, who lived nearby. Although Mrs. Rollock was active in the various causes to which Cora Calhoun Horne had devoted much of her life, she did not share her late friend's strict attitudes about the upbringing of a teenage girl. She paid for dancing and singing lessons for Lena and was happy to allow Lena to entertain girl friends in her home. She also had less stringent requirements concerning the companions Lena chose, and Lena was able to enlarge her circle of friends, first at PS 35 and later at Girls High School in Brooklyn. Lena dared to feel secure in her identity and in her community, to feel as if she could put down roots at last.

Soon, however, she was uprooted once more. After sending Lena back to Brooklyn, Edna Horne had gone on the road again and had visited Cuba on tour. There she had met and married a white Cuban named Miguel ("Mike") Rodriguez, and when Lena was fourteen Edna proudly showed up with her new husband and announced that they were going to be a family again.

Initially, they settled in Brooklyn, but the insular black middle-class community did not welcome them. There was a strong antiwhite prejudice among the Brooklyn black bourgeoisie, and Mike's attitude only made the situation worse. He had an abrasive personality and an open contempt for American Negroes who, he charged, were responsible for their second-class status because they refused to fight back against racism. In Lena's view, Mike's only redeeming quality was his fiercely protective attitude toward her mother.

The Great Depression that had followed the stock market crash in 1929 was firmly entrenched by now, and Mike couldn't find work. Their lack of money, coupled with their lack of social acceptance in Brooklyn, led them to move to the Bronx, where Lena was thoroughly unhappy. She didn't like the school she attended and made no friends there. She attempted to remain in contact with her Brooklyn friends, but the distance made it difficult. With few social outlets, she was forced to remain in the apartment with her parents in an atmosphere that was increasingly strained.

Like many other adults she'd known, Lena's stepfather blamed her whenever her high-strung mother became upset, and he constantly scolded her. When he wasn't scolding her, he was railing against the American economic system that deprived him of a job. Lena hated his thick Spanish accent, the way he had taken over as the boss in their lives, and the disparaging remarks he made about American blacks. And as their financial situation grew bleaker, she blamed him for not being able to find a job to support her and her mother properly. Before long, they were unable to afford the apartment in the Bronx and were forced to move to a run-down Harlem tenement. In exchange for the apartment, Mike worked as unofficial superintendent of the building, but though he tried he could not make either the apartment or the building livable. For food, they were forced to rely on relief organizations. Lena must have recalled that not very long before, she had lived in Mrs. Rollock's comfortable home, had taken dancing and piano lessons, and had her girl friends in for tea and cookies. She had belonged to a service sorority called the Junior Debs and had thought nothing of requesting a new party dress for the benefits at which the girls served as hostesses. During the time she had lived with Mrs. Rollock, she had found herself longing to be part of a real family, but she didn't consider the arrangement in which she was living with her mother and stepfather a real family situation. She enjoyed no respect from her stepfather, and her mother was so overcome by their terrible financial situation that she seemed concerned only about herself.

By the time she turned sixteen, Lena had concluded that her family life was virtually intolerable, but she entertained no serious thoughts of leaving. The earlier beatings and the more subtle appeals to her capacity for guilt about her mother had thoroughly indoctrinated her, and she could not bring herself even to voice her unhappiness to her mother for fear that she would upset the older woman. Nor could she stand up to her stepfather, for she feared his volatility and knew instinctively that he would some-

how manipulate the situation to her disadvantage. She did, however, begin to think seriously about going to work herself.
Although she had no skills to speak of, she had one marketable
asset: her looks.

Her own self-concept was too dismal for her to see herself as
beautiful, but she was aware that other people regarded her as
such. She heard the whistles and catcalls as she walked down the
street. At least once, as an adolescent on the road with her mother,
she had been the object of sexual advances by an older man. She
was tall, slim, light-skinned, had "good" hair, and she was young.
Even in the midst of a depression, there was a market for such
assets.

Lena's beauty had not gone unnoticed by her mother and
stepfather. Lena's mother, in particular, had begun to transfer her
own dreams for a successful career in show business to her daughter. She hadn't wanted Lena to be exposed to the seamier sides of
an entertainer's life when she was still so young, but at length she
realized that they couldn't afford the luxury of protecting her from
the real world any longer. They needed the money she could earn.

Lena doesn't recall who brought up the subject of her working.
As she remembers, it was a decision arrived at almost simultaneously by everyone. And once it was brought up, there was little
discussion before it was unanimously agreed that she would.
Money was uppermost in everyone's mind, but for Lena there
were other advantages. She could leave a school that she hated
anyway, she would have somewhere to go besides the depressing
apartment and its tense atmosphere, and perhaps, if she did
become the major breadwinner in the family, she would be
entitled to some respect.

2

TALL, TAN, AND TERRIFIC

ONCE the decision had been made that Lena would go to work, her mother decided immediately that Lena would not slave in black stock companies nor be subjected to the grueling life of on-the-road tours. No, she would aim higher for Lena right from the start. In fact, she would aim for the top, and in those days the top for a girl as inexperienced and untrained as Lena was the chorus line of one of the big, whites-only Harlem clubs like Connie's Inn or the Cotton Club. Edna chose the Cotton Club because she had a connection there—she had met Elida Webb, dance choreographer for the club's big shows, years before and had maintained the contact in case she ever needed it. Through Elida Webb, she arranged for Lena to audition for the club's chorus line.

It was a very brief audition. Lena sang a few bars and danced a few steps and was hired. Talent was not paramount in Cotton Club chorus girls; a certain "look" was, and Lena had it. The white patrons of the club liked to see light-skinned, straight-haired, beautiful, and *young* girls perform in the abbreviated costumes for which the line was famous, and Lena qualified on every point.

There was rejoicing in the dingy Harlem apartment that night. Not only had Lena landed a job on her first try, she had gotten a job at the famous Cotton Club, a place that Edna considered the pinnacle of success and that Lena found equally impressive. As far back as she could remember, the Cotton Club had represented the ultimate in glamour. When she was living with Mrs. Rollock, she had listened to live radio broadcasts of the shows from the club and had never dreamed that one day she would be part of those shows. The club's legend, which would live long after the club itself, was firmly entrenched by the early 1930s; and if the club's heyday had already passed, this fact was not yet recognized by most observers.

The Cotton Club owed its existence to the Volstead Act and that odd period of American history called Prohibition. With the banning, in 1919, of the sale of all alcoholic beverages, except those required for medicinal purposes, the United States of America became "wetter" than it had ever been before. Large segments of the population began to see drinking as *de rigueur,* whereas before the passage of the Volstead Act they would not have thought much about imbibing. The mere fact that they were not allowed to drink turned a lot of Americans into consummate drinkers. With the increase in demand, willing suppliers stepped in to fill it. Previously unorganized criminals now organized to provide bootleg liquor to a thirsty public; their marketing and distribution were the epitome of American entrepreneurship. Nationwide, hardly a community existed that did not have some solid pipeline to a spiritous source.

In New York, the passage of the Volstead Act happened to coincide with another odd period of history called the "Harlem Renaissance." Post-World War I migration of Southern blacks to the North helped to spawn a large concentration of blacks in places like Harlem. This concentration, in a comparatively liberal city, inspired a creative tension among talented black writers and musicians—a celebration of blackness. Meanwhile, whites who longed for creativity and who possessed wealth had the luxury to identify and bemoan the miasma of white culture in the aftermath of World War I, and once they discovered blacks they imbued them with all the innocence and natural feeling that they were certain the white culture had lost. They looked to the expanding population in Harlem, caught the sense of excitement there, and suddenly discovered black writing, music, and dance. If Dr. Alain Locke, a black, had not coined the term "New Negro," no doubt some white writer would have. Whites of a certain economic, intellectual, and social class began going up to Harlem to see this New Negro in his native habitat, and whites of a decidedly different intellectual and social, though not necessarily economic, class saw a brand-new market.

Owney Madden never went to college and didn't get rich until Prohibition, but he was a smart enough businessman to see a new market. To this former denizen of Hell's Kitchen, where he had earned the nickname "Owney the Killer," it was logical that wealthy whites with cravings for both bootleg liquor and things "New Negro" would flock to an exclusive Harlem night spot where they could observe the natives without having to mingle with them. From Sing Sing prison, where he had been sentenced in 1912 to a ten-to-twenty-year term, he directed his lieutenants to come to an agreement with Jack Johnson, the black former heavy-weight champion, under which his second-floor Club Deluxe on the northeast corner of 142nd Street and Lenox Avenue would be turned into a posh, segregated nightclub, with white patrons and black entertainers, that would not only pay its own way but also serve as a principal outlet for his "Madden's No. 1 Beer." Jack Johnson would be allowed to front for the operation until he could be eased out.

Madden was paroled from Sing Sing for good behavior in January 1923 and could have been present at the grand opening of the Cotton Club in the fall of that year, but he preferred to maintain a low profile in connection with the club. He was a businessman, not a club operator, and he had hired people to run the club who had far more expertise in that line than he. The

27

shows were based on the all-Negro revues that had been so popular on Broadway since the advent of *Shuffle Along* in 1920; the admissions policy was strictly segregated; and the black entertainers were either superbly talented or beautiful or both. Before long, anyone who was anybody made a point of going to the Cotton Club; the shows rivaled the downtown revues for energy and glamour; and some of the most talented white songwriting teams were creating memorable music specifically for the Cotton Club shows. Once the Madden gang relaxed their policy of hiring only Chicago-based employees, musicians, and entertainers in 1927, the club also became a showcase for the best black talent in the country, and nationwide radio broadcasts of live Cotton Club shows could be heard weekly. For whites, the Cotton Club became *the* place to go, at least once, and an obligatory stop on any tour of the city for foreign or domestic dignitaries. For blacks, it became *the* place where black talent could be showcased to a nationwide audience.

By the time Lena joined the Cotton Club chorus line, the Volstead Act had been repealed, the "New Negro" had lost some of his exotic appeal, and the Depression had curtailed the frivolities of many of the club's former patrons. But the name of the club still spelled magic, and the club's star was only slightly tarnished. Its very existence was still anathema to the Brooklyn black bourgeoisie, who were scandalized when they read in the local black newspapers the press releases that Lena's mother had made sure to send out to every paper she could think of. Lena Horne a Cotton Club girl? How utterly shameful! If Edna was taken aback by this reaction, it was only for an instant; she had already been effectively ostracized for marrying Mike. Lena had a similar reaction; she had lost touch with her Brooklyn girl friends, she was a world away from them, and what was the point in caring how they felt? She had a job at the famous Cotton Club; her girl friends were probably secretly green with envy.

If Lena had believed that landing a job at the Cotton Club would mean a modicum of personal independence, she was wrong. Her mother accompanied her to the club the first night she reported for work and nearly every night thereafter. The Cotton Club girls had to exist in very close quarters as it was—crammed into a small dressing room and discouraged from using the club's only ladies' room, which was reserved for the white patrons—but Edna plunked herself down on an available chair and sat through show after show until it was time for Lena to go home. She didn't just sit, she lectured; Lena was not to talk to male employees, nor was she to exchange more than superficial pleasantries with the female employees. Lena was to be *with* the other girls in the chorus line, but not *of* them, for the others were sophisticated, worldly, and older than she, and they would certainly teach her lessons that her mother did not want her to learn.

While it was true that the other girls counted among their unofficial duties entertaining favored customers and were indeed far more worldly, Lena never felt that they would have tried to coerce her into behaving as they did. In fact, she believed that they would have protected her. When she first arrived, they had gone out of their way to make her feel welcome. But Edna's constant, forbidding presence had angered them, and soon they began to resent Lena for being "special." They ignored her, and she felt the familiar sense of not belonging.

She resented her mother's presence. She realized early that she wasn't in danger of being asked to "entertain" after hours, in private, as the other girls were, because she was too young. At sixteen, she was jailbait, and even the most lascivious-minded boss at the club was unwilling to risk the club's license by offering to even the most important patron the favors of a girl who was under the legal age of consent. Besides, Lena felt capable of protecting her own virtue, having acquired a keen sense of irony about the sexually charged atmosphere in the club and about the silly contrast her mother presented. Every night, three shows a night, she went onstage in skimpy, sexually enticing costumes, and as soon as she returned backstage she had to listen to a moral lecture from her mother.

Anyway, she didn't need her mother's protection. She already enjoyed more protection than her mother could give; that protection came from her father and his friends.

By the time Lena went to work at the Cotton Club, the rigid color bar had been relaxed to accommodate important black Harlem gangsters, of whom Lena's father was a member in good standing. Though they were usually ushered to out-of-the-way booths by the kitchen, they were nevertheless allowed in, for they were business associates of the Madden gang and their connections were sufficiently important to override general rules. As soon as Lena joined the chorus line they were there, assuring her that they would watch out for her, that they were friends of her father's. Lena much preferred their background presence to her mother's nagging.

Lena found her work at the Cotton Club grueling. She worked three shows a night, seven nights a week, plus obligatory political functions at any time, for a salary of $25.00 a week. This salary was docked whenever she missed or was late for a show or a rehearsal. She had to pay for her own meals—food at the Cotton Club was served to the patrons, not to the employees—and the money she handed over to her mother and stepfather on payday was never enough to do more than maintain the family at a slightly higher level of nourishment than they had existed on before. Although $25.00 a week was half again the salary earned by a store clerk or a stenographer, it had to stretch far to accommodate three people. It did not afford them the opportunity to move from the Harlem tenement to a better apartment, and thus Lena and her mother and stepfather had to continue their uncomfortable sleeping arrangement, under which someone always seemed to wind up sleeping on the couch because the one bed in the apartment was in use, and under which tired people moved somnolently from couch to bed whenever the one bed became free. The biggest problem, in Lena's opinion, was that although she was indeed the family's major breadwinner, she was not winning bread in sufficient quantity to ensure her parents' respect. They still treated her like a child. But her mother and stepfather had become more cloying and apparently more intent on maintaining a hold on her.

While Edna's purported reason for accompanying Lena to the club every night was to protect her daughter's chastity, she enjoyed being around the stars who performed at the club. Her husband did, too, and since neither of them had a steady job, they had the time to spend at the club. Mike appeared to enjoy criticizing the club's black employees and entertainers for allowing themselves to be exploited by the management; he boasted that Lena would not be exploited as long as he was around, although, except for not being asked to entertain favored customers privately, Lena worked under the same conditions as the other girls did.

It was indeed an exploitative arrangement. The entertainers' salaries were lower than those paid white entertainers at downtown white clubs, and their working conditions were poorer. Although all the entertainers were black, the producers, the choreographers, and the songwriters who worked on the shows were white, a situation that thoroughly rankled veteran black entertainers like Flournoy Miller, who worked fairly steadily as a comedian at the club. Miller, in conjunction with his vaudeville partner, Aubrey Lyles, and with the vaudeville musical team of Noble Sissle and Eubie Blake, had been responsible for the writing, arranging, choreographing, and producing of *Shuffle Along*, the first black musical to reach Broadway. Its opening to rave reviews there in 1920 is credited by many as the beginning of the Harlem Renaissance. Miller longed to work on the production end of one of the Cotton Club's shows, but he was never given the chance.

Black entertainers played the Cotton Club because it was famous and because its transcontinental radio broadcasts enabled them to reach a wide audience. The club's owners and managers also had connections and would recommend entertainers and bands they liked. Many of the big-name black bands, among them Duke Ellington's, got their start at the Cotton Club. Other bands like Claude Hopkins's and Jimmy Lunceford's were willing to play the Cotton Club dirt-cheap because the opportunity to bill themselves as "formerly of the Cotton Club" was an automatic ticket into other clubs across the country. The same was true for individual entertainers, not just the stars but members of the Cotton Club Girls and Cotton Club Boys. But they paid a lot of "dues" at the club, not just by accepting low wages and cramped dressing rooms and acceding to club policies against free food and drink, but by accepting their sometimes tacit and often overt treatment as a subclass of human being.

Lena was only dimly aware of the resentment toward the club management felt by the other entertainers. She heard them grumble and shared their unhappiness over the long hours, the lack of independence, and the low pay, but she was a star-struck teenager who felt so fortunate even to be at the club and to be near the stars she admired that she had little inclination to ponder the injustices of their situation.

Her first show at the club, in the fall of 1933, headlined Cab Calloway and his band. She had met Calloway before, having been a Junior Deb hostess at a benefit where he and his band performed back in Brooklyn, but she did not expect him to remember her. When he immediately spied her and called out, "Hey, Brooklyn!" she felt a rush of both pride and humility. She would always be grateful to him for recognizing her and helping to make her feel at home in an alien place. She was also impressed to appear in a show with Ethel Waters. To Lena, even the other Cotton Club Girls represented the height of glamour and sophistication, but her mother's insistence on protecting her virtue from their sordid influence prevented her from developing any friendships.

Actually, she had no close friends at all. She worked with adults, and her odd hours were not conducive to her meeting people her own age. Her Brooklyn friends were now not just geographically distant but a world away in experience and life-style. As had happened so often in her past, Lena was a stranger in her own world.

As a rule she was too tired to worry about that and too caught up in the excitement of working at the club to think about where she might go from there. She had no clear aspirations to advance in the world of show business and was quite content to remain a chorus girl. But her mother and stepfather were impatient for her to have a featured spot in one of the shows, and they nagged the shows' producers constantly. They also enlisted the help of Flournoy Miller, whose advice the producers would occasionally deign to take informally. Thus, when Lena was offered the opportunity to fill in for a girl who suddenly quit a featured number, she didn't know if the producers really wanted her or if they just wanted to shut up her unofficial cheering squad.

The number was part of the spring 1934 Cotton Club Revue, and it featured dancer Avon Long. Long and a partner sang and danced to "As Long As I Live," written by the famous songwriting team Harold Arlen and Ted Koehler, who were veterans of the Cotton Club shows. Lena was well received as Long's partner and was subsequently offered another featured part with the Claude Hopkins band; she sang a duet of "Cocktails for Two" with a male singer who was part of Hopkins's group. Since Lena had no formal voice training she would often get hoarse by the end of the night, and her mother decided she needed voice lessons. Although the fee for these lessons took a chunk out of the $25 a week on which the entire family lived, Lena's mother and stepfather believed it was a worthwhile investment in her increasingly promising career.

As a result of her feature performances, Lena came to the attention of Lawrence Schwab, producer of a show called *Dance With Your Gods* that he planned to take to Broadway. The thin plot line centered around voodoo and witch doctors and would star the respected black actors Rex Ingram and Georgette Harvey. The part that Schwab had in mind for Lena was a minor one, described only as "A Quadroon Girl," and he was not so much interested in her talent as in her beauty and appropriate skin color. Lena's mother and stepfather didn't care what kind of part he had in mind—he was talking about Broadway.

33

The management of the Cotton Club also didn't care what kind of part Schwab was talking about. They pointed to the contract Edna had signed which forbade Lena to take any outside jobs while she worked at the club. No amount of ranting on Mike's or Edna's part would budge them, nor would Schwab's more considered arguments. At length, he approached Broadway organized-crime contacts of his own, who interceded with the Cotton Club mob and secured an arrangement whereby Lena would miss the first show at the club in order to appear in the play.

Unfortunately, *Dance With Your Gods* closed after only a few weeks, and Lena barely got her feet wet as a stage actress. The director of the play assured her she had potential, and with this encouragement Lena's mother and stepfather began to agitate against the iron-clad contract that was stifling her opportunity to grow as a performer.

By this time, the Cotton Club mob was thoroughly sick of Lena's whole family. Sure she was young, and pretty, and nubile, and the customers liked her, but there were plenty more where she came from. And her numerous potential replacements would not have troublesome mothers and stepfathers as part of the package. Moreover, the mob didn't like being challenged, particularly not by some unemployed, abrasive Cuban. One night Mike was beaten and his head stuck into a toilet bowl, and even he had sense enough to stay away from the club after that.

There was no question, now, that Lena would leave the Cotton Club. But the family couldn't afford to lose her salary. Flournoy Miller stepped in and offered a chance for escape. His friend and fellow producer of *Shuffle Along*, Noble Sissle, was in Philadelphia with his band and needed a singer. Miller arranged for Lena to audition. Secretly, she and her mother traveled to Philadelphia, where Lena sang "Dinner For One, Please James" and was hired, not so much because she displayed any great talent as a singer but because she had been sent by Flournoy Miller—and, of course, because she was gorgeous. Her one physical imperfection, according to retired actress Frances Williams, bothered Sissle not at all. Williams recalls, "I met Lena in 1940-41, at Rockefeller Center in

New York, where Noble Sissle and his orchestra were playing. Noble introduced me to her and she was just beautiful, radiant. And then she walked away and I looked . . . and said, 'Aw, isn't that too bad.' She was bowed from the hips down, and her face was so pretty. Noble said, 'Doesn't matter, baby, she sings in a long dress.' She's covered it well all these years.''

One wonders if the rickets Lena suffered as a child affected the development of her legs.

Once a new job for Lena had been assured, she, her mother, and her stepfather packed quickly and literally fled New York and the Cotton Club mob.

3

ESCAPE FROM
THE ROAD

THE Noble Sissle Society Orchestra was among the more successful black orchestras of the time. Sissle's press releases reminded
potential bookers that he and his U.S. Army band—black
contingent—had made a substantial contribution to the morale of
U.S. and Allied troops overseas during World War I. And as one
of the four writers/producers/directors/performers in *Shuffle
Along*, he had a substantial following. At a time when most black
bands worked sporadically, he and his group performed with
considerable regularity, although they had to travel a lot in the
process. Sissle was clever enough to know that the key to attract-
ing a big audience was to alert the local NAACP and the local
black press, and these important organs and organizations of the
black community never failed to respond, not only with substantial publicity and special functions in his honor, but also with the
necessary stamp of approval conferred by members in good standing of the black bourgeoisie. In fact, the Noble Sissle Society
Orchestra was so acceptable that it even occasionally played for
whites.

Noble Sissle himself was bourgeois, and thus he understood that in hiring Lena Horne as his singer he was also taking on her mother and stepfather. Lena was only eighteen, and, though Sissle demanded a modicum of decorum from the members of his orchestra, he did not particularly want the responsibility of chaperoning her. Still, he had expected that Lena's relatives would make some effort to fit themselves into the band's routine and its established mechanisms for coping with the inevitable racism they encountered on the road. They were accustomed to conducting extensive searches for lodging in black sections of the towns where they played, to settling for poor accommodations, to taking food from the back doors of restaurants, and to sleeping on their tour bus when they couldn't find suitable lodgings. With the arrival of Mike Rodriguez they were forced to examine their customs a little more closely than they cared to.

Having recovered from his beating at the hands of the Cotton Club mob, and being safely away from New York, Mike was as abrasive as ever when he joined the Sissle tour; he was also as critical of black Americans' reaction to their poor treatment. Uninvited, he would hold forth on conditions for blacks whenever he had the opportunity. He was seemingly unaware that his presence increased the group's difficulties even in finding accommodations in black neighborhoods. Black hotel and boarding-house keepers were not especially pleased to offer lodging to him, although they generally did so because he was with the Sissle group. He was particularly insufferable whenever the group encountered discrimination from whites.

Not long after Lena and company joined the Sissle Orchestra, the group had the opportunity to be the first black orchestra to perform at the Ritz-Carlton in Boston. For Noble Sissle, who had been touring for years without such an opportunity, this was important, and he didn't want anyone in his entourage to mess up—or to be messed with. On the way to Boston he lectured his band members on dignity and decorum and, aware of the presence of Lena and her mother, if not also of the presence of Mike Rodriguez, he made some rather risky pronouncements about his intentions to uphold the dignity of the black woman in the face of whatever potential indignities the group would encounter.

When, on arrival at the Ritz-Carlton, Sissle and his band were informed that they must enter and exit the hotel by way of the kitchen, not only the dignity of the black woman, as represented by Lena and her mother, but the dignity of Noble Sissle suffered, and a gleeful Mike was quick to point that out. There had never been any question that the group would have to find living quarters outside the hotel; Sissle had hoped only for the largely symbolic freedom to lead his band through the front door.

Life on the road with the Sissle band meant a constant experience of racism. For Lena, it also meant the tension of feeling responsible for her stepfather's abrasiveness and for her mother's unhappiness, which lifted only when Lena was onstage and living out her mother's dreams. The conditions of living on the road played havoc with Lena's voice, as did the practical considerations of being a band singer. Lena used her voice more than she ever had. She sang an opening duet with Sissle and another featured number with male singer Billy Banks. She also sang ballads in the show, among them "Blue Moon" and "Old Fashioned Love." Meanwhile, she wasn't even sure she was a singer, although with Noble Sissle she began to enjoy singing and to regard her voice as a finely tuned instrument that needed care if it was to perform properly. She did know that she liked entertaining an audience, responding to it and feeling its response, and she thoroughly enjoyed the work of the band and felt proud to be associated with it. She understood, as her stepfather never would, that the Noble Sissle Orchestra believed that the opportunity to make music and to perform far outweighed the sometimes distasteful circumstances in which they were forced to pursue their art.

When Lena had been with Sissle for close to a year, the orchestra set out on a Midwestern tour that made the tour in the East seem comfortable by comparison. In the Midwestern towns where they played there were no sizable black communities and thus few friendly boardinghouses or restaurants. Their tour bus became their hotel, and when, in Terre Haute, Indiana, they were forced to spend the night on the grounds of the Clyde Beatty Circus, the tension of the tour and the ill-feeling that existed between Mike Rodriguez and the members of the Sissle Orchestra came to a head. Mike blew up and so, at last, did Noble Sissle. He ordered Lena's stepfather to leave the tour, and an oddly surprised Mike turned in his figurative meal ticket and returned to New York.

Edna was left in a quandary. For all his rudeness, Mike was her husband; he had at least stayed with her and supported her, and she had become very dependent on him. But she couldn't leave Lena, who was yet a teenager and whose virtue she had sworn to protect. Edna stayed with the tour, promising Mike that she would visit him whenever she could.

The next stop after Terre Haute was Cincinnati, where the band was to experience another first: no black band had ever played at Cincinnati's Moonlight Gardens before. They had already been informed that no blacks would be admitted to the audience, and they were prepared to use whatever second-class entrance the Moonlight Gardens had. Noble Sissle frequently traveled by separate car, finding it easier to study arrangements and conduct the business of the orchestra in private. On the way to Cincinnati he was in an accident. The tour bus arrived well ahead of the car in which Sissle was traveling, and it was hours before his entourage learned that he was laid up in a hospital in Delaware, Ohio.

Sissle was not so seriously injured that he couldn't foresee the implications of his absence for his band. The band would have to have a substitute conductor, one who would catch the imagination of the press and the public. From his hospital bed, Sissle directed that Lena take over as conductor and that during her tenure as bandleader she be known as Helena Horne, which he believed sounded more sophisticated.

Since Noble Sissle had already written all the arrangements for the band, all Lena/Helena had to do was wave a conductor's baton at appropriate intervals. She gamely rose to the occasion, the band paid absolutely no attention to her, and opening night in

40

Cincinnati was a big success. In fact, the Noble Sissle Society Orchestra got its best reviews in the Midwest while "Helena" Horne waved the conductor's baton and the band followed the first trumpet. The recuperating Sissle started thinking about ways to exploit the obvious audience appeal of his young singer.

The next stop after Cincinnati was Cleveland, and Lena's father drove up to see her from Pittsburgh, where he was living with his second wife and operating a hotel, the Belmont, that included a gambling room called "The Bucket of Blood." He visited only briefly, and Lena longed to see more of him. After completing its booking in Cleveland, the Sissle Orchestra was scheduled for a few days of rest, and Lena wanted to spend it with her father. Her mother was also tired of touring and anxious to see her husband, and she put up little argument. While Lena visited her father, Edna would be able to go back to New York and Mike.

Thus, Lena found herself free of her mother for the first time in years, as she traveled, chaperoned by a member of the Sissle Orchestra, to Pittsburgh. There she was welcomed by her father and stepmother and treated not as a child but as a grown-up guest. Teddy Horne took his daughter to nightclubs and dance halls and to all the places where he rightly suspected she had performed but had not enjoyed as an ordinary patron.

A young friend of Teddy Horne's often accompanied them. Louis Jones was young enough to be Teddy's son, but they shared mutual interests, among them card-playing for money. Louis Jones was the son of a minister and he was college educated, but he was keenly interested in politics and very ambitious, and no doubt he saw that Teddy Horne, who had a hotel and a successful "numbers" business in Pittsburgh, could be of help to him. Once he met Teddy Horne's daughter, Lena, he hung around even more.

Louis Jones was nine years older than Lena, but the age difference didn't bother her; she was accustomed to living in a world where everyone else was older than she. What attracted her was his politeness and his respectfulness, his refinement as compared to the men she was used to being around. She'd been looking for a

41

man who was respectable and not in show business, although she wasn't sure just how long she'd been looking for someone with these qualities. She only knew that she wanted to escape the domination of her mother and stepfather and that for a long time she had realized that the life of an entertainer was not the "normal life" for which she yearned. For her that normal life included a house and a yard like the ones she'd known on Chauncey Street in Brooklyn, children, and a sense of roots and belonging. It might also include singing from time to time, but that wasn't terribly important to her. Lena wasn't committed to her "art." She had become an entertainer out of necessity, and that was what she continued to be. At first, she had performed to pay the bills; now, she performed because, she suspected, she was living out her mother's dream of stardom. What she herself wanted was some control over her own life, and at the age of nineteen she decided she could have it by marrying.

Louis was equally interested in marrying Lena. He saw in her youth and beauty the perfect adornment to his life, and he also wanted a home and children. By the time Lena left Pittsburgh to rejoin the Sissle Orchestra, the two were determined to marry as soon as possible.

When Edna learned of these plans, she was furious. She pleaded with Lena to reconsider, and since that didn't work, she pleaded with her ex-husband to talk their daughter out of her decision. But though Teddy Horne didn't approve of the marriage—he wouldn't say why—he refused to interfere in his daughter's life. Noble Sissle was willing to try to talk Lena out of the idea; he didn't want to lose her, and he believed she was making a mistake in forsaking her career for marriage. But Lena wouldn't listen to him, and since she wasn't under formal contract with him he had no hold over her. Lena returned to Pittsburgh to be with Louis.

They set a wedding date a few weeks hence and traveled to New York to collect the belongings Lena had left there. In New York her mother, who had left the Sissle tour when Lena had, and her stepfather tried again to talk her out of the marriage. They were certain she was ruining her life. Lena, however, believed she had never had a life. She wanted independence and a chance to be conventional.

Lena and Louis were married in January 1937, in the living room of her father's and stepmother's home on Wiley Avenue. Lena wore black, for she felt it was a sophisticated color and somehow symbolized her new independence. She had no idea of the responsibilities that were in store for her, having thought only about the imagined freedoms.

She did not, for example, know how to cook. Her mother had made a point of keeping her as far away from the kitchen as possible, not wanting "kitchen work" to spoil her good looks. She was naïve about money, and she soon learned that she and Louis had very different ideas about it. They didn't have enough money to afford a home of their own and lived the first few months of their marriage in the home of one of his brothers. Yet Louis had expensive tastes and continued to indulge them after the marriage. They were often in debt, and if Lena's father hadn't stepped in frequently to bail them out, they would have been hounded constantly by bill collectors.

Lena also didn't know how to provide the emotional support her husband expected from her. Louis, though a graduate of West Virginia State College, was unable to find a job that suited his abilities. The best job he could get was clerking in the county coroner's office, and even this position was a reward from the local Democratic machine for his work for the party. Daily, he suffered indignities as a black man, and when he got home he wanted sympathy and support from Lena. But Lena was feeling too resentful when he did come home to do anything but nag him. Louis believed that his only chance for real success was to work tirelessly for the Democratic Party and its potential benefactors. Many nights he was out doing ward heeling. He didn't share his political business with Lena. Even when he had political meetings at home, he expected her to serve refreshments but otherwise to be as unobtrusive as possible. On the nights he attended his bridge club he would take her along, but he didn't want her to play.

When Lena complained that she was cooped up in the house all day he offered to teach her to drive. But the lessons proved to be disastrous. Louis was so impatient with her and so critical that Lena chose not to learn, and to this day she cannot drive a car. Apparently, at least in their inability to teach someone close to them, Louis Jones and Teddy Horne were alike.

It took Lena only a few short months to realize that she had made a mistake in marrying Louis, that instead of gaining the freedom and independence she had wanted, she'd merely stepped into a different trap. She might seriously have considered leaving Louis if she hadn't become pregnant almost immediately. She looked forward to having a child and hoped that it would bring her and Louis closer together, for she didn't know how else the two of them would reconcile their grave differences.

Treated throughout her pregnancy by a black doctor, Lena naturally assumed that he would also deliver her child. But when she and Louis and her stepmother arrived at the local hospital, her doctor was waiting on the steps to inform her that he couldn't accompany her inside. Although the hospital had a small ward set aside for black maternity patients, black doctors weren't allowed to practice there. Lena tensed up immediately and became increasingly more rigid as cold, white strangers attended to her. She was in labor for two days, but at last her daughter, Gail, was born. Lena left the hospital vowing never again to be subjected to the inhumanity she had suffered during one of the most important events in her life.

After they'd been married for a few months, Lena and Louis had moved to a rooming house. With the arrival of Gail, they moved into a house of their own, and Louis's sister came to stay with Lena to help with the baby. Lena enjoyed having company, and she enjoyed taking care of Gail. She also liked the idea of having a real house, although it seemed that the most consistent visitors were bill collectors. If it had not been for their serious financial problems she might not even have considered the movie offer she received when Gail was only a few months old.

Harold Gumm, an agent in New York, called to offer her a role

in an independently produced musical starring Duke Ellington
and titled *The Duke Is Tops*. Filming was due to begin in Hollywood soon, and as it was to be a "quickie musical," shooting
would take only about ten days. Lena initially felt that she
couldn't leave Gail so soon, but Louis persuaded her to accept the
offer. They needed the money. He also insisted that she have a new
dress to wear to Hollywood, even though the purchase put them
deeper into debt.

In Hollywood, shooting on the film began as scheduled. Lena
played the wife of Ralph Cooper, a featured actor in several
previous independent films and a former emcee at the Apollo
Theatre in Harlem. The rather thin plot line centered around the
two show-business careers of the husband and wife, and shooting
was planned to take such a short time because there were to be
numerous production numbers, some of which were already on
film. Unfortunately, like most independent films, and like most
of the few films featuring blacks in this era of the late 1930s, the
budget was of the shoestring variety. Hardly had filming begun
when Lena and the rest of the cast were informed that their salaries
would not be immediately forthcoming.

When Lena called home to tell Louis that she wouldn't be paid
right away, he demanded that she leave the show and return to
Pittsburgh. Lena refused. She explained to her husband that
entertainers who were true professionals didn't forsake a show
just because they didn't get paid on time. None of the other actors
were leaving—there were so few roles available to blacks in films
that they were willing to work for promises rather than pay. Lena
stayed, over Louis's protests. Filming was completed on schedule,
but Lena never did receive her full salary. Louis was furious.
When the picture premiered in Pittsburgh, the local chapter of the
NAACP held a special benefit showing and attempted to honor
Lena, but her husband wouldn't allow her to attend.

Once Lena had told him that she wouldn't be paid right away,
Louis made several calls to the New York agent, Harold Gumm,
to demand her salary, even though Gumm had protested that he
didn't control the budget of *The Duke Is Tops*. That experience

should have soured Gumm on Lena, but apparently it didn't. In the fall of 1938, not long after *The Duke Is Tops* was released, Gumm called again, this time to offer Lena a part in a Broadway revue, Lew Leslie's *Blackbirds of 1939*. Lena hesitated even to broach the idea to Louis and was surprised when he readily consented. No doubt he saw another chance for Lena to earn money, and perhaps he was secretly excited about the world of show business, although he sometimes made pronouncements about "sinful" show people that betrayed his upbringing as a minister's son.

This time Lena took Gail and a babysitter with her. Lew Leslie found lodgings for them and was, in Lena's opinion, particularly nice to her. At first, he seemed to want to find in her a reincarnation of Florence Mills, the famous black star who he had produced in the 1920s and who had died, tragically, of acute appendicitis in 1927. Once he realized that Lena was nothing like Florence Mills, he began to pay attention to her for herself. He introduced her to his family and included her in family outings. He was similarly fatherly with other members of the cast, partly because he, too, was having trouble raising the necessary money to produce the show. Lena and the others received lodging and meal money, but they saw no salary checks. Tryouts of the show in Boston garnered poor reviews and thus no money for new investors. The members of the cast chose to stay with the show, and it did manage to open in New York. Louis came up from Pittsburgh for the opening night, but he wouldn't allow Lena to attend the cast party afterward even though Lena particularly wanted to go to it. She and everyone else involved felt that the very fact that the show had managed to open was cause for celebration. Nonetheless, she acceded to her husband's wishes once again. The show stayed alive for only eight nights, and Lena, Gail, and the babysitter returned home, Lena having gained little more than experience.

By the time she returned to Pittsburgh, Lena was furious with Louis for his lack of understanding of a professional entertainer's life, for his assumption of the right to tell her where she could and could not go, and for all his other shortcomings as a husband. She was so bitter that she didn't even want to be in the same house with him, and she immediately went to her father for help. She wanted him to finance her freedom and was dismayed when he refused. While he hadn't approved of the marriage to begin with, Teddy Horne had no intention of underwriting its demise.

He did arrange a family meeting at which he and Lena's step-mother and Louis's family urged Lena and Louis to try to make a success of their marriage. Reluctantly, the young couple agreed. Lena had no other choice, for without money she couldn't sup-port herself and Gail. Resignedly, she went through the motions of being a wife and was shortly pregnant again.

This time Lena chose a white doctor, who would not be forced to abandon her on the steps of the hospital at delivery time. Edwin, called Teddy, and named after her father, was born in 1940, a little more than two years after the birth of Gail. Not long after the birth of his son, of whom he was inordinately proud, for Teddy was the first Jones grandson, Louis told Lena that if she ever left him she would not get Teddy. Apparently, Lena hadn't been the only one who had felt little but resignation after the family meeting.

For a while immediately after Teddy's birth Lena didn't allow herself to think about leaving Louis. She had little time to think about herself at all while caring for her infant son. But in unguarded moments, Louis's threat came back to her, and she began to formulate a plan that would enable her to be independ-ent of him.

She received help from an unexpected quarter—one of her husband's fellow bridge-club members. Charlotte Catlin played the piano at private social affairs, and she suggested that Lena join her. Louis approved of the idea because of the high social class of the people for whom Charlotte played. Lena was able to regain some of her confidence as a performer with Charlotte. The dismal experience she'd had with *Blackbirds*, and Louis's con-stant denigration of her ability to make money in the entertain-ment field, had caused her to lose whatever confidence she'd had.

Meanwhile, Lena took steps to ensure that she would have the

47

money to finance her escape, should she ever get the courage to undertake it. She secured her stepmother's promise that if she came to the point where she could no longer live with Louis she would be eligible for a loan that would pay her way to New York and support her until she could support herself.

All that remained now was for Lena to gather the strength to leave her husband. Some of it came from her renewed confidence in her ability to make it on her own; some of it came from the assurance that she would have a financial base; and some of it came from her awareness that the tension in her marriage was beginning to affect Gail, who was old enough by now to detect the undercurrents of bitterness and resentment that Lena and Louis betrayed. But it appears that Lena needed a climactic act of betrayal on Louis's part to galvanize her to action.

Such an act was not long in coming. While Louis was preparing to leave on a political trip, Lena discovered that he had hidden a pair of handmade shoes under the living room couch. The money he had paid for these expensive shoes could have paid several of their past-due bills; worse still, he had clearly tried to hide them from her. She went into a rage that surprised not only her husband but also herself, for she'd never before given vent to her bitterness so freely. She promised to leave, but Louis didn't take her seriously. He left on his trip as planned. While he was gone, Lena arranged for a woman to live in the house and care for Gail and Teddy; Lena then collected the loan promised by her stepmother. By the time Louis returned, she was all set to go. He reminded her that she would never have Teddy, but Lena refused to allow even the fear of losing her son to dissuade her and, promising to return for *both* her children when she had established a new home for them in New York, she left.

4

SHE'LL TAKE
MANHATTAN

LENA Horne arrived in New York to reestablish herself in show business and to begin her life as an independent woman, in the fall of 1940. She had already enjoyed a fairly substantial career for a black entertainer, having played at the Cotton Club, sung with a major Negro orchestra, appeared twice on Broadway, and made a Hollywood film. She had been married and separated and had borne two children. She was twenty-three years old.

For all her experience, she felt singularly ill equipped to succeed in New York. She realized that she lacked an education and had felt that lack keenly during her years in Pittsburgh. Louis and his friends seemed to know so much more than she, and Louis's manner had caused her to feel insecure about her ability to do almost anything. She also was completely unaccustomed to being alone and fully responsible for herself. She arrived in New York a veritable stranger, for her mother and Mike had gone back to Cuba. She made contact with a few old friends in Brooklyn, but as she explains, "My people in Brooklyn are like people in Washington and Philadelphia and they tend to cling together, they tend to be cliques, and I was still out from all of that."

All she really had going for her, besides her looks and her former career, was her will, and perhaps to bolster that will she immediately checked into the Hotel Theresa on 125th Street and Lenox Avenue in Harlem. Only recently integrated, it was a posh hotel by any standards, and certainly by the standards of Harlem. Having settled into her suite, she donned the fashionable suit her stepmother had bought her in Pittsburgh and went around the corner to the Apollo Theatre, where any black entertainer who was anybody appeared at least once a year. Although Noble Sissle and his orchestra were not on the Apollo's bill at that moment, she imagined she could find out where he could be found. But Noble Sissle was out of town, and the managers of the Apollo couldn't suggest another band that needed a singer. Jobs were as tight as ever for black entertainers; even the chorus line at the Apollo was filled. Secretly relieved that she didn't have to take a job "hoofing" again, Lena graciously accepted the managers' offers to let her know if they heard of a lead.

Having exhausted the possibilities uptown, Lena swallowed her pride and called Harold Gumm, the downtown white agent who had suggested her for the role in *The Duke Is Tops* and the part in Lew Leslie's *Blackbirds of 1939*. But Gumm could offer little help, for although he had contacts in a number of fields, none of those fields held fertile ground for black performers at the time. In the theater, the heyday of black shows was over; indeed, there was a certain backlash underway, a reaction to the relatively substantial black presence during the Harlem Renaissance and later, during the WPA Federal Theatre period. Black theater had gone back to the community, to little-theater productions and independent ensembles, none of which had the commercial viability that Lena needed. In Hollywood, the pickings for blacks were as slim as ever, and Gumm had received few calls for black actresses of Lena's "type." In music, the situation was similar; the black bands that could afford them already had singers, and few white bands would take on black singers. The clubs that featured black singers were blues and jazz clubs, and Lena didn't sing the blues.

The problem for Lena was that she didn't quite fit—anywhere. In particular, she didn't fit the stereotype of a Negro. One producer after another was pained to tell her that she was too light-skinned, too straight-haired, too something. Producer George White told her that her best tactic would be to pass herself off as Spanish, and Harold Gumm agreed with this advice. Angry, Lena told them they could keep their advice and went back to Harlem, where she accepted an invitation to appear at a benefit at the Apollo. She needed the exposure, and she needed to work. Noble Sissle and his orchestra also performed at the benefit, and Lena asked Noble for her old job back; but Sissle and his group were experiencing some hard times of their own; he couldn't afford to hire a female singer.

Lena's funds were getting low. She moved out of the Hotel Theresa and into a room at the Harlem YWCA on 135th Street between Seventh and Lenox Avenues. Since there wasn't much to do, she spent a lot of time listening to the radio and learning songs that she might add to her repertoire. Among her favorite popular hits was "Stardust" by Artie Shaw, and when she was feeling lonely and needed to talk to someone—anyone—she called the disc jockeys and asked that the tune be played. Eventually, she was forced to go to work at a movie house—the Victoria Theatre on West 116th Street—and it was there that she was located by Clarence Robinson. The dancer and choreographer for the shows at the Apollo had made good on his promise to keep her in mind for possible jobs, and when Charlie Barnet called to say his singer was ill and he needed a replacement in a hurry, Robinson went looking for Lena.

Charlie Barnet was white, and so were the musicians in his band, but he was a musician's musician and had performed at the Apollo to appreciative black audiences. Barnet wasn't averse to hiring a black singer, but except for Artie Shaw, whose lead singer was Billie Holiday, he was alone in his lack of racial preference. Lena auditioned and was immediately accepted. Bob Carrol, the male singer with the band, later recalled that she did the next show without any arrangements and "stopped it cold." Even so, Lena had misgivings. She worried about how to act around white musicians, how it would be to tour with them, and how her father would react to her singing with a white band. Her father didn't like it, and Lena would have chosen practically any other band-singing job in preference to the one with Barnet's band; but she needed the money and she needed to work.

Almost immediately, the band and its new black female singer went on the road, and soon Lena felt professionally comfortable with Barnet and his group. They cared far more about their music than about skin color, and they treated Lena more as a fellow musician than as a pioneer of sorts. Barnet regarded Lena's voice as an instrument and had songs specially arranged to suit it, emphasizing its strengths and improving its weaknesses. Her range was not wide, nor did she have much power, but she was good with a lyric and was capable of infusing some fairly mundane verbal phrases with a modicum of meaning. She was best at popular songs, and while with the band she recorded "Good For Nothing Joe," "Haunted Town," and "You're My Thrill," all on the Bluebird label.

She got along well with the band members socially, too, for many of the men were interested in a lot more than her voice. While Lena, at this time, was hardly interested in a relationship with any man, much less a white one, the men were not about to give up on possibilities, and being surrounded by amorous admirers was an advantage for Lena when she encountered personal discrimination that Charlie Barnet was as powerless to stop as Noble Sissle had been.

Hotels that had been pleased to accept advance reservations for the white Charlie Barnet band changed their minds when they saw that Lena was part of the group. Usually, Barnet canceled the reservations and searched for a hotel that would take his entire ensemble. Lodging was only one of the problems. There were places the band appeared where Lena was accepted as a performer but not as an onlooker—it was okay for her to get up on the stage and sing, but when her song was over she couldn't sit onstage between numbers with the musicians. This was unacceptable racial mixing. When there was no powder room for Lena to wait in, she waited on the bus; and if it wasn't parked too far away from where they were performing, members of the band would keep her company. All these were problems that the band suffered *above* the Mason-Dixon line. When the band made preparations for a Southern tour, Charlie Barnet was rational enough not to try to take Lena along. He gave her a paid "vacation," which she spent with her stepmother on a steamboat cruise down the Mississippi. During that cruise, she decided not to rejoin Barnet and his band. She appreciated the support she'd received, but she didn't feel like going on "paid vacations" when the band played where she couldn't. She was tired of feeling guilty when, because of her alone, the entire group had to look for another hotel or Barnet had to rearrange his stage show to allow time for her to get to and from the bus between her numbers. Besides, she felt that she had been away from her children too long. She had been with Charlie Barnet only six months, but she had saved her salary, and she believed that it was enough to start the home for her children that she had envisioned. Her father, who initially opposed her working with a white band, had softened his stand somewhat; he understood that she was just doing what she had to do. But as an incentive to quit, he had offered her the house on Chauncey Street, which he had inherited. Lena now had a house and money for food and clothing. All she needed was someone to take care of Gail and Teddy. After saying good-bye to Charlie Barnet and his musicians, she went to Chicago, talked a Horne cousin named Edwina into moving to New York to take care of the children, and returned with her to get the Brooklyn brownstone ready to house a family again.

When Lena arrived in Pittsburgh to claim her children, she felt a certain sense of victory, for she had done what she had set out to do: earn enough money to establish a home for herself and Gail and Teddy. Louis had told her she couldn't do it, and she'd proved him wrong. But Louis still had his ace up his sleeve, and he used it. Teddy wasn't going anywhere—Louis had made that promise when his son was an infant. Lena, for all her dreams about a family on her terms, respected the wishes of her husband. Although she wondered if Louis wasn't simply using Teddy to hurt her, she had too many memories of losing her own father to demand that Teddy leave his. She returned to New York with Gail alone, having made arrangements with Louis to have Teddy part of the time.

Returning to New York, Lena was ready to resume her career with far more credentials than she could boast when she had arrived in the city from Pittsburgh. She had promised Charlie Barnet when she left the band that she would appear with the group when they played the Paramount Theatre, and her appearance on the same bill as the popular white singer, Dinah Shore, brought her exposure. "Good For Nothing Joe," which she had recorded with the Barnet band, had become a hit. She was more beautiful than ever, and that, too, gave her entrée into the New York music world. In addition, she was dating Joe Louis. She attracted the attention of John Hammond, among others. A talented musician, Hammond had found his real calling as a manager and "packager." He brought Count Basie and Billie Holiday together; he was another pioneer in uniting the worlds of black music and white music, which before the 1940s were entirely discrete. He had a particular interest in bringing the two worlds together at Café Society Downtown, a club owned by Barney Josephson who, like Hammond, was color-blind when it came to music and entertainment. Josephson, who also owned and operated a club called Café Society Uptown, had no hang-ups about who could patronize his clubs and who could perform in them, except that the performers had to be real jazz or blues singers and that his patrons must really appreciate what they were hearing. Lena Horne uses the term "chauvinistic" to describe the musical tastes of Barney Josephson and his patrons: "They were purists, and to me that's a little selfish, because I was not a blues singer, and I was not a good jazz singer. I think I'm the first hybrid that ever went to work for Café Society, because it was known for jazz—marvelous, real jazz."

Ordinarily, John Hammond wouldn't have suggested Lena to Barney Josephson, but Hammond says he got a frantic call from her. She said she was sick of being chased up and down hotel corridors by musicians—couldn't he get her a job as a single? After a time, Hammond thought about Café Society for Lena. "She had never worked with a small jazz band, and my interest in the club was best served by giving performers like her a chance to be heard with the best accompaniment," he wrote in his autobiography. He also wanted to help business at Café Society, and he was shrewd enough to realize that her beauty, and the presence of Joe Louis, would do that.

Hammond recalls that at the sight of Lena, Barney Josephson forgot about being a jazz purist. Overwhelmed by her beauty, he took her hand and said, "Miss Horne, I have to tell you something. You're so beautiful, you have such class, we can't let you be called Lena Horne. Would you mind if I changed your name to Helena Horne?"

Hammond's recollection notwithstanding, Lena had been renamed Helena once before—by Noble Sissle. But there is no reason to question the impression she made on Barney Josephson or his feeling that anyone as beautiful as she ought to have a more appropriately beautiful name. Three weeks after he hired her, Josephson, believing that if he was so deeply affected others would be, too, sponsored a concert for Lena at Carnegie Hall, and as he had expected she was eagerly received. Business at Café Society Downtown picked up immediately. The downtown club had not been doing well since the opening of the uptown branch. Critics had charged that "the heart of what made Café Society a mecca for hep-cats and Villagers" had been "cut out and shipped uptown." With the arrival of Lena there was an infusion of something popular and marketable, although it was certainly not "heart" in the sense that jazz and blues buffs meant it. Lena's upbringing and background had not prepared her to sing the kinds of songs that the patrons of the original Café Society had come to expect. Barney Josephson and others were determined to change all that, however.

Commuting from Brooklyn to Greenwich Village via the BMT subway line, Lena thought at first that she was just going someplace to sing. It did not take her long to realize that she was also in for an education. Barney Josephson, so taken by her beauty, might have forgotten himself for a moment, but he was not about to let her be beautiful and unenlightened. The lessons actually started right at her audition. She sang "Sleepy Time Down South," and almost immediately Josephson interrupted her, asking her what she thought were the implications of the song. Lena hadn't thought about the implications—it was a currently popular song. Josephson pointed out that it maintained myths of Southern black contentedness that she ought to know weren't real. Lena thought about her childhood experiences in the South and her recent experience of not being able to go on tour there, and she realized that Josephson was right. She also felt ashamed and angry that a white man had been the one to point out the irresponsibility of singing the song. But it was hard to stay angry at Josephson. After hiring her, he made it a point to be her instructor in black history, political references, and a great many other things that she'd never thought about before. And because Café Society Downtown, located in Greenwich Village and with a liberal admissions policy, was a center not just of music but of ideas, she found herself in the most intellectual atmosphere she'd ever experienced. If she'd thought herself dumb in Pittsburgh, it was nothing compared to how she felt now. But the people she met at Café Society Downtown seemed eager to help her learn. Under the tutelage of Barney Josephson and others, she began to learn about Afro-American history, about politics, about social structures, about who she was in relation to the world around her. She looked at these predominantly white, predominantly well-educated, would-be teachers, and felt resentment and an impulse to run away; but far stronger was her eagerness to learn, even if only to dispute them, and so she began to listen carefully and to read. She read voraciously and widely. She read African history and Afro-American history and world history. She read as if possessed, because she wanted to make up for her lack of education and for the years she had been working instead of going to school. She acquired the habit of reading to relax, of reading at meals when she was alone, of reading whenever she had the opportunity. At first she read because she wanted to catch up, because she wanted to know what the people around her were talking about. Gradually, she settled into the habit of reading for herself alone and not as a response to others.

Lena's history lessons during her stint at $75.00 per week at Café Society Downtown also included personal history. One night Paul Robeson and Walter White came in. Both of them had known her grandmother.

Paul Robeson was a legend then. His portrayals of characters in Eugene O'Neill plays, among them *The Emperor Jones,* had established him in the 1920s as the leading black dramatic actor; his subsequent work in musicals and in concerts in America and Europe had established him as the most famous black American entertainer in the world. Walter White was executive director of the NAACP. "So I met two heroes the same night," Lena recalls, "and they both had known my grandmother and they told me about some of the bad things as well as the good."

Lena had been a teenager when her grandmother died, and her memories of Cora Calhoun Horne had been fraught with conflict. She had listened at the meetings her grandmother had forced her to attend and had even been aware that when her grandmother was hard on her, it was to teach a lesson of some kind. But she was young then, and it hadn't seemed to her that what her grandmother had to teach was important. It had seemed to Lena that from her grandmother's point of view one only had to work hard and be committed in order to succeed. Her grandmother never let her know that the working and commitment could be done from any other environment but Brooklyn and the Harlem streets where Cora Calhoun Horne had worked. Lena had felt constrained and constricted by her grandmother; she'd resented her strength and her power over Lena's grandfather, Edwin, and the rest of the family.

Paul Robeson and Walter White presented a different idea of Cora Calhoun Horne to Lena. She hadn't known that her grandmother had helped Paul Robeson get a scholarship to Rutgers University. She hadn't known that her grandmother graduated from Atlanta University when she was sixteen years old and worked to "bring her children to a free land where they had not known what she had known." Lena listened, fascinated. "The only thing I regret," she said years later, "is that she never told me all the bad things that she had known. She kept me in the future always."

Lena kept this personal education to herself. "Nobody knew about my people, in Café Society, except those two," she says. "I was hungry to hear all that." The thoughtful pride she was developing about her family and her roots was enhanced by her relationship with Joe Louis, whom she began to date while in New York and whom Barney Josephson considered another "plus" in Lena's favor, for Louis attracted people to the club. Lena was with Noble Sissle and his orchestra when Louis was defeated by Max Schmeling, and she and the band members had gathered around a radio between sets to listen to the fight. Every one of them cried when Louis lost, and Lena's mother had been disgusted with the lot of them, refusing to understand that for most black people Louis was an important symbol and that his defeat somehow represented a defeat for the entire race. In 1939, Louis beat Schmeling, and he was the man of the hour when he and Lena began to date. His victory was claimed by most blacks as a personal victory, and Lena was proud to be seen with him.

Lena's musical education continued at Café Society. Teddy Wilson led the small jazz band at the club, and Lena credits him with teaching her a lot. "I had no inborn sense of rhythm; I couldn't count a thing. And Teddy began to work on just following the lines. Then I began to pick up this kind of thing. I wasn't singing great at all, but I was learning also how to work with an audience. That's where the first of it began." The drummer, J. C. Heard, helped her, too, and so did the other singers who enjoyed the easy, pleasant atmosphere of Café Society. White singer Mildred Bailey, black singers Hazel Scott and Billie Holiday (Holiday, though extremely vulnerable herself, took a protective attitude toward Lena and scolded her if she was seen with any man whom Billie considered not up to her standards) encouraged her and advised her. Lena recalls, "All were giving, giving to me, and I was soaking it up."

She learned that she was most comfortable around musicians; their racial tolerance and sense of democracy appealed to her, and knowing them helped her to overcome some of her own racial prejudices. But she also learned from talking with the busboys and waiters and other ordinary workers at the club. She had never been a part of the ordinary working world, and until then she had not thought about the fact that "all my people had to work like dogs." Now that she had a child to support (Teddy was with Louis) and was a working woman, she began to understand what those who labored in a less rarified atmosphere had to deal with every day.

While she was at Café Society, Lena's fame began to spread. She was a featured singer on NBC radio's *Strictly For Dixie* show and appeared regularly on WOR radio's *Kats and Jammers* show. During this time she also appeared in a twelve-minute film with Pete Johnson and cut two albums for RCA Victor titled *Birth of the Blues* and *Moanin' Low.* Her effortless vocal delivery and her beguiling beauty propelled her into New York prominence, and she was happy with her success.

She was also happy in her personal life. Very family-oriented, perhaps because she had missed having a family life as a child, she was comparatively surrounded by family during this period. Her uncle Frank was now living in Washington, DC, where he served as an informal adviser to President Franklin D. Roosevelt, and he visited often. Her uncle Burke was now manager of the Apollo Theatre. Gail had made friends in Brooklyn and seemed happy there, and for some reason Louis had decided to allow Teddy to visit her, although the visit was not as long as she had hoped it would be.

Thus, when Harold Gumm, who only a year or so earlier had advised her to pass herself off as Spanish, came to her with an offer to go to the West Coast, her initial reaction was to refuse. The engagement was at a big, new club in Hollywood called the Trocadero, and for its grand opening Felix Young, the owner, had planned a bill that included Ethel Waters, Duke Ellington, and the Katherine Dunham dancers. Lena felt honored to be asked to join the company of such stellar performers. Further, Gumm suggested that the exposure she would receive at the Trocadero would lead to film offers. But Lena was not sure she wanted to jeopardize the stable existence she was enjoying.

Lena pondered the benefits and drawbacks involved in a move to the West Coast. She would have to uproot Gail, and she was not sure she ought to. She would be farther away from Teddy, her uncles, her father and stepmother. Her brief experience while filming *The Duke Is Tops* had shown her that Hollywood was a white town and a racist town; she wasn't sure she could handle living there. She knew she would miss the intellectual stimulation of New York, and she realized that she wouldn't learn as much about music, particularly jazz, in Hollywood. For these reasons, among others, Barney Josephson urged her to decline the offer. He said she would be crazy to go, and Lena agreed with him. "I don't want to go to Hollywood," she said. "I don't want to make any more movies. Forget it, I'm happy here."

But Teddy Wilson and the guys in the band felt differently. They told her she had to go. She was being given the opportunity to become a big star. And Walter White also urged her to go, although for different reasons. He was certain that Lena's exposure at the Trocadero would lead to movie opportunities for her, and he saw her as a tool to break the racist syndrome that confined blacks in Hollywood movies to roles as servants, comics, or natives in jungle movies. He believed that she had the strength to resist that stereotyping, to demand less demeaning roles, and to inspire other black actors and actresses. White's powerful arguments persuaded Lena to try to be a pioneer in Hollywood. She realized she would be sacrificing her own happiness, but she felt a sense of mission. She wanted to put into practice the ideas she had learned in New York. Before her departure, she sought the blessing of Barney Josephson, whom she considered a good friend, but Josephson would not be mollified. He told Lena he wouldn't guarantee her job back at his club if she returned from Hollywood. Then he walked away from her in silence. Although saddened by Josephson's reaction, Lena refused to be dissuaded from her mission. With Gail and cousin Edwina, she moved to the West Coast in early 1942 after only seven months at Café Society Downtown.

5

FROM PILLAR TO POST

ACCORDING to veteran actress and little-theater manager Frances Williams, it was she who suggested Lena for the Trocadero. "I was working with Katherine Dunham, trying to get her ready to open at the Big Troc on Sunset Strip," she recalls. "Felix Young was actually trying to open two clubs, the Big Troc and the Little Troc, and Katherine had a big revue planned for the big club. She asked if I knew anyone who was pleasant-looking, with a fairly good voice; she'd decided that she needed that kind of single to open with her. I remembered Lena from New York, when she was with Noble Sissle, and I thought she was just the kind of person Katherine wanted. So Katherine sent for her."

The Japanese had attacked Pearl Harbor and restrictions on building materials had been immediately imposed, so Felix Young was having a hard time getting the Big Troc ready. Lena, who had borrowed the money for her West Coast move from her father, was worried when she learned on arrival that there was no job waiting for her. She couldn't afford to be idle for long.

Felix Young was aware of her plight and, feeling responsible for temporarily stranding Lena and her family, took it upon himself to find her an apartment and to see that the rent and food bills were paid. But in his well-meaning efforts, he made the mistake of renting an apartment in an all-white section of Los Angeles, on the coincidentally named Horn Avenue, which proved to be welcoming to Lena only in name. The neighbors did not take notice when cousin Edwina, who was so light-skinned that she could easily pass for white, arrived, but Lena and Gail were clearly of suspect hue. In order to avoid the neighbors' questioning looks, Lena spent most of her time inside the apartment.

Hollywood was a lonely place for Lena at first, and it could have been positively dismal if Duke Ellington hadn't been there when Lena arrived. He was doing a show called *Jump for Joy*. Ellington invited Lena to be a guest performer and she eagerly accepted, not enjoying her enforced idleness while waiting for the Trocadero to open. He introduced her to Billy Strayhorn, whom Ellington had told her back in New York she ought to meet. Strayhorn not only played in Ellington's band but was his chief music-writing collaborator. He was also his friend, and, in introducing Lena and Billy, Duke was less interested in Lena's friendless Hollywood condition than he was in Billy's sexual preferences. Strayhorn was gay, and back then homosexuality was viewed by most of the population as a disease of some sort that could be cured by the right woman. Unfortunately for Duke's plans, Billy, who was called "Swee Pea," and Lena took to each other in every way but sexually. Billy was not interested in women, and Lena had been so indoctrinated by her mother's Victorian ideas about sex that she was hardly about to try being passionate in an effort to turn him around. However, their personalities and their ideas about music seemed to mesh. They could sit talking for hours, and Lena found herself opening up to him, confiding hopes and fears that she had never told anyone before. At other times they made music together, Billy creating arrangements for her and helping to keep her voice in shape. "We did everything together . . . walking on beaches, talking, talking about things we read or heard or saw, going to pictures, everything together," Lena told Maurice Zoloton in an article in the November 1982 issue of *Los Angeles* magazine. "I loved him . . . I would have married him if we could have married." But the relationship could not go beyond the sharing of mutual likes and dislikes into intimacy. Even so, their closeness would remain. According to Zoloton, when Strayhorn lay dying of cancer years later his only request was "to spend his last days with Lena."

Though she had her friendship with Billy Strayhorn and the settling in of her family to keep her busy, Lena was anxious to start working, and thus when Felix Young announced that he simply could not open the big Club Trocadero and that the show planned for the club would have to open at the Little Troc instead, Lena was ready to sing on a street corner. The entire extravaganza opened in February 1942 at the smaller club, which was much too small for the lavish show prepared by Katherine Dunham and her troupe; her dancers needed space for their re-creations of ethnic ceremonies. "But," says Frances Williams, "it was just right for Lena."

Lena stepped out onto the stage wearing a simple white dress and illuminated by one soft light. Without introduction and without even announcing her number, she began to sing. In the cozy, intimate atmosphere of the club her listeners felt as if they were hearing familiar songs for the first time. Soon, they were calling for more—"Blues in the Night," "The Man I Love," "Embraceable You," "My Bill," "Can't Help Lovin' That Man." She sang eight numbers in all, and left the crowd wanting more.

In Frances Williams's recollection, Lena's energetic agent (Harold Gumm had followed her to Hollywood to look after her business arrangements) had a perfect selling point. "He dressed that club with Victor Mature, Rita Hayworth, all the people in his stable and everyone else's, and *made* Lena Horne. I mean, she was the toast of the town. People almost forgot Katherine was there."

Before long, anyone who was anybody considered it de rigueur to be seen at the Little Troc and to have seen Lena Horne. People who never went to nightclubs pushed their way in four or five nights a week to hear her. Buddy de Sylva was one who went there to hear her sing and was quoted as saying, "She's the best female singer of songs I've ever heard. It's how she sells them. I sat there and listened to her sing 'Somebody Loves Me, I Wonder Who.' She gives lyrics a new meaning. She puts something into a lyric that even the author didn't know was there. I ought to know, for I wrote the lyric to 'Somebody Loves Me, I Wonder Who.'" But most people went to *see* Lena. Her style of delivery, accepted as part of her act by the more sophisticated audiences at the Café Society Downtown in New York, was viewed as pure and unmitigated sensuality by Hollywood audiences. In Hollywood's eyes, she was the embodiment of the primitive, the exotic—the "New Negro" of the Harlem Renaissance gone West. It didn't occur to most of Hollywood that she might be a normal person when she wasn't performing.

Hollywood's leading hostesses began to invite her to parties, because it was the daring thing to do, but she soon realized she was being used. Being the target of racist remarks from a few Hollywood leading ladies was only part of it; she realized in short order that, unlike the other guests, she was expected to sing for her supper. After Duke Ellington and Billy Strayhorn left town with their show *Jump for Joy*, she was particularly lonely and in need of acceptance, but after a time she decided she preferred being lonely to being used. A few hosts were cordial and eager to hear her sing just for the sake of it, and when Lena was in a good mood she would kick off her shoes, sit down, and sing well into the night. At parties where she felt she didn't belong, she kept her shoes on and her singing to herself, and after a time she began to refuse most invitations. She felt that, if she was to be a sex object, the sex-objectifiers could get their enjoyment without her cooperation.

Lena's father came out to visit her soon after she opened at the Little Troc, and she enjoyed the opportunity to be with him. He'd go to the Little Troc to hear her sing, then take her out to a black after-hours club to listen to blues music (Lena found to her regret that there was no good jazz being played on the West Coast then). As an adult, Lena had come to know and respect her father as she hadn't had an opportunity to do as a child, and while she regretted the time she'd missed with him, she was all the more grateful for their late-blooming relationship. She was especially glad to be able to call on him for advice, which she found she needed when having been in Hollywood barely two months she learned that she was wanted for the movies.

George Raft, who she had met at the Cotton Club, came to hear her at the Little Troc and subsequently arranged a screen test at Universal Studios for her. But Lena credits Roger Edens with "discovering" her. He was a musician and a songwriter for films and was in Hollywood working for Arthur Freed, a producer at MGM. He'd heard Lena at Café Society Downtown, went to hear her again at the Little Troc, and believed she ought to be in pictures. Harold Gumm, to whom Edens first broached the idea, wasn't licensed to handle movie contracts, but he secured the aid of the Louis Shurr agency in the person of Al Melnick, who was even more energetic than Gumm. The day after her Universal test, Lena auditioned at MGM.

That audition was a coup for Melnick, who had virtually camped on Arthur Freed's doorstep in an effort to persuade the producer to hear her sing. Probably more interested in getting rid of Melnick than in hearing Lena, Freed finally agreed to let her sing for fifteen minutes. But once he had listened to her, he wanted to hear more. She sang for two hours. Then Freed took her in to sing for Louis B. Mayer, who was entertaining actress Marion Davies in his office at the time. When Lena had invested two more hours of singing she was offered a contract.

Even though she had nothing but praise for Al Melnick, Lena wasn't about to sign any contract without some advice from family and friends. She was a bit overwhelmed by the reception at MGM, and suspicious of the excitement she had generated. While Mayer himself had been noncommittal, Freed and Melnick were promising that great things were in store for her. She didn't want to get caught up in the excitement and make a wrong move. She called Walter White, who happened to be in Hollywood then, to ask his advice about the opportunity. White's concern was that Lena would be cast in maid or jungle native roles; he urged her to be firm in demanding a contract that would enable her to be offered roles that were dignified. She also called her father and asked him to come back to California to help her negotiate her contract, for she valued his judgment and business savvy. When Lena arrived at MGM to negotiate her contract, she was accompanied not only by her agents but by her father, who was as insistent as Walter White that Lena not be relegated to undignified roles. As he informed the people at the studio, he could afford to hire a maid for his daughter if she wanted him to; she was not going to play any maids. Under the terms of the seven-year contract that Lena eventually signed, she was guaranteed an initial salary of $200 per week and would not be asked to play any of the traditional, stereotyped roles that strangled the broader talents of other black artists in Hollywood at the time. MGM was planning to produce a couple of all-black movies, including a film version of *Cabin in the Sky,* which had done so well on Broadway, and there was a solid role available for Lena in this film.

Lena left the MGM offices feeling that she had begun to do what she had set out to do in Hollywood: pave the way for other blacks to get some respect from the studios. She would soon learn that by acting independently she had incurred the ire of many in the black community in Hollywood, a group as tightly knit and insular as the Brooklyn black bourgeoisie. It didn't matter to them that she was the first black woman since 1915 to be signed to a term contract by a motion picture company and only the second black woman in history to be signed to such a term contract (Madam Sul-Te-Wan had been the first, signed by D. W. Griffith in 1915). What mattered to them was that she had not played by established rules.

The rules were overseen by a group of veteran black actors in Hollywood who acted as bosses in the black acting community and who had formed a sort of unofficial union of black performers. Although the "members" of this union paid no dues and carried no union cards, they relied on the good graces of the "union bosses" to get them work. Under the very strict, but informal, system, studios that needed black actresses and actors for films would get in touch with the bosses, who in turn would suggest the names of favored friends. So efficient was this system in a town where roles for blacks were few, that the major studios didn't have to sign black actors to term contracts; they could use the established, and far less costly, route. Since most parts for blacks in Hollywood were those of extras, the bosses could always be relied on to provide a few actors for a few days, at day wages, rendering unnecessary the sort of contract that Lena had signed, which called for her to be paid a maintenance salary even when she wasn't working. But the bosses did not understand how they, and the black actors and actresses in their "stable," were being used, or if they did, they saw no alternative to it. When Lena took her independent and principled stand they were upset by the potential destruction she could cause to their tiny sphere of influence. They called her an "East Coast upstart" and a "tool of the NAACP"; and it was made known to Lena that in their view, she was not a pioneer, but a traitor.

Lena was shocked by this reaction on the part of her own people; her previous experience had been that black people got jobs and protected them through racial solidarity. It took time for her to realize that this custom did not operate among the majority of black actors in Hollywood, who were not musicians or singers or others with particular talents. As she explained in her autobiography, "Plenty of people wanted their jobs, irregular as they were, and the kind of acting they did was not beyond the power of almost anyone. They were mainly extras and it was not difficult to strip down to a loincloth and run around Tarzan's jungle or put on a bandanna and play one of the slaves in *Gone with the Wind*. It seemed significant to me that the people who had real talent . . . did not join in the attacks on me."

Among these people with real talent were Eddie "Rochester" Anderson, and Hattie McDaniel, with whom Lena became quite close. Hattie McDaniel had won an Academy Award as Best

Supporting Actress for her portrayal of the Mammy in *Gone with the Wind*, and she had suffered from the traditional Hollywood stereotyping. She supported any move to achieve some dignity for blacks in films. But Hattie McDaniel was an established star, with over twenty films to her credit; most other black actors and actresses had neither the luxury nor the temerity to buck the traditional system over which the bosses ruled.

Social ostracism by the comparatively small population of black actors in Hollywood was not easy for Lena to take, especially when she was new to the area and virtually friendless in an overwhelmingly white, racist town.

Once she started to make some money, Lena moved her family East on Horn Avenue across the Sunset Strip to a better, and she hoped more friendly, neighborhood. Unfortunately, some of the people in the new, comparatively upper-class section were equally unfriendly. They took up a petition to oust Lena from the neighborhood. More liberal-minded neighbors, among them Humphrey Bogart and Peter Lorre, quashed the movement. Lena never met these actors socially when they all lived in that neighborhood. Other, less well-known neighbors, supported her, too. Lena particularly remembers a French family next door who she later discovered received frequent visits from Greta Garbo. Eventually she was invited to meet the woman who was one of her favorite actresses. She remembers little about Garbo except that she was "all eyes and had the most beautiful bones." The support of some of her neighbors didn't, however, erase the reaction of the others from Lena's mind.

Not long after she signed her contract with MGM, Lena had her first chance at a movie role, undergoing a screen test with Eddie "Rochester" Anderson for a film called *Thank Your Lucky Stars*. The script called for a black couple who were servants to a white couple; the parts were not stereotypical in the old vein because the black couple had some realistic dialogue. Eddie Anderson was already set to play the husband, and Lena expected to be offered the role as his wife. But in the screen test, Lena photographed too white next to Anderson, a contrast that was taboo in Hollywood films—it would offend white moviegoers. Lena thought this taboo pretty silly, pointing out that Negroes came in all shades, but she did not protest when the MGM makeup department was ordered to develop a shade of makeup for Lena that would make her appear darker and closer to Anderson's color. The makeup department did indeed create a shade for Lena that approximated Anderson's complexion; unfortunately, it made her look as though she was in blackface. The producer decided not to cast Lena as Anderson's wife and gave the part to Ethel Waters, who did not need a lot of makeup to match his color. Lena thus lost her first major film role, and, though she did not know it, her only chance to appear in a speaking role in a mixed-cast picture for thirty years.

If Lena hadn't been under contract with MGM, the problem of making her up to look "Negro" might not have been so serious. But since she was under contract, something had to be done. Eventually, cosmetics king Max Factor was called upon. He created a shade for Lena that he called "Light Egyptian." The unfortunate result of this development was that it could be applied to white actresses, relieving MGM of the necessity of finding mulatto actresses to play mulatto roles. Lena herself would eventually lose parts to white actresses because of this new dark makeup.

Not long after her screen test for *Thank Your Lucky Stars,* Lena was cast in a nonspeaking part as a singer in an otherwise all-white film called *Panama Hattie.* The movie starred Red Skelton and Ann Sothern, but Lena never got an opportunit to work with the two stars. Her number was staged and shot separately, and the segment was no doubt an afterthought, planned as a way to give her something to do in return for her salary and perhaps also to give Vincente Minnelli an opportunity to show what he could do. Minnelli, the film's dance director, had worked as a Broadway art director and was known for having a "flair for the exotic." He directed Lena in a Latin-flavored song-and-dance version of "Just One of Those Things" with the Berry Brothers, a well-known

71

dancing team, and he and Lena became good friends. Lena was not pleased with her performance in the number. Accustomed to singing in front of small orchestras and combos, she gasped when she faced a huge orchestra with fifty violins. Her voice was drowned out. Removing sixteen of them helped, but Lena had an idea that MGM felt she'd let the studio down.

The film, which was released in 1942 only weeks after Lena's number was shot, was forgettable. Those who saw it in its unedited version felt that Lena was the best thing about it. Wrote critic Harrison Carroll, "Best production number in the picture features the sultry Negro singer, Lena Horne." Those who saw the edited version of the film had no opportunity to assess Lena's talent, for they did not see her at all. In keeping with the prevailing custom, MGM had arranged the production so that Lena's number with the Berry Brothers had no integral meaning to the thin story line and could be easily excised in copies of the film that were sent to Southern movie theaters and to theaters in other parts of the country where white moviegoers would find a segment featuring blacks offensive.

Ironically, some blacks who saw the film charged that Lena was trying to "pass" as a Latin, although she had nothing to do with the type of number she did. Some whites evidently believed she was Hispanic, and MGM received inquiries regarding its new "Latin" discovery. When the studio got such inquiries about Lena, its PR people referred to the biographical information form for which Lena had supplied some scanty facts. Here are some of the answers she gave:

Father's occupation: hotel owner
What studies best in: music, dramatics, history, literature
Nearest relatives (brothers, sisters, etc.): (says none)
How often attend picture shows: once a week
What would do if out of pictures: stage and radio
Convictions regarding stage and screen—do they conflict? likes
    both
Childhood ambition: to be on stage

Favorite actor is: Chaplin (screen)   Evans (stage)
Actress: Bette Davis (screen)   T. Bankhead (stage)
Favorite motion picture is: *Mutiny on the Bounty*
Stage play: *Barretts of Wimpole Street*
Do you govern your life by any rule or rules? no
Any superstitions? never hope too hard—never pans out
Believe in hunches? yes
Details if ever successfully followed a hunch: had a hunch to
     leave good job in New York and come to Hollywood, then
     landed a better job.
Hobbies: reading—any type book
Favorite recreation: dancing—music

Among the several questions Lena chose not to answer were
"Opinion of Hollywood" and "Outstanding impression of Hollywood." She knew that her honest opinions wouldn't look good
on the MGM form.

In Lena's next film, *Thousands Cheer,* an otherwise all-white
movie that starred Mickey Rooney, Judy Garland, and Dick
Powell, she struck a pose that was to become her trademark
through the 1940s: singing while leaning against a pillar. The
image of Lena, always elegantly gowned, singing while draped
around a marble column in a lavishly produced musical sequence, would become virtually standardized. Only her ability to
appear enigmatic prevented her from being completely exploited
in these stock sequences; she managed to carry them off with a
dignity that, coupled with her aloof and detached delivery,
enhanced both her mystery and her audience appeal.

Lena had been in Hollywood only a few months; already she
had been a smash at the Little Troc, and then gone on to repeat her
success at the Macombo, where she'd opened in July, had a movie
contract and had shot singing sequences in two movies. But she
missed New York and was hungry for news from the city she
considered her home. Thus, when she learned that a benefit was to
be given at Café Society Downtown, she decided on an impulse to
go. She had time because filming still hadn't begun on *Cabin in
the Sky.* Both Arthur Freed and Vincente Minnelli wanted that

project to be as carefully crafted as possible, given that an all-black musical was a risky venture. Lena was so eager to get back to New York, even for a couple of days, that she was actually willing to fly—her least favorite form of transportation.

She recalls that on arriving in New York, "I went to the Theresa, left my bag, and went to Birdland. Basie was playing there, Charlie Barnet was at the bar; even Billy Daniels was there, I think, all the musicians, and I walked in and I started to cry, and I said, 'I'm never going back there again.'" Only on seeing her friends and being back in New York did she realize how very much she had missed it all. Duke Ellington, Billy Strayhorn, Hazel Scott, Billie Holiday—all the friends she cared about most were based in New York.

Billy Strayhorn and Billy Daniels escorted Lena to the benefit at Café Society Downtown. In the months since she had left, Barney Josephson had gotten over his anger at her leaving; the two kissed and hugged like long-lost friends, and Josephson assured her that she was welcome to sing or just to visit at Café Society whenever she was in town. After the benefit, Lena and her two escorts went out on the town. They caught Count Basie's show at Birdland and afterward Basie joined them for more club-hopping. By evening's end, Lena was feeling sentimental and, having drunk a lot of champagne, more than a little tipsy. She blurted out, "I'm back where I belong, I'm never going to leave New York again."

Basie reacted immediately. He got her out on the street and informed her that in the morning he was going to "send her buns back to Hollywood. Because that's where you have to go."

As Lena told Gil Noble on ABC-TV's "Like It Is" in 1981: "He said, 'They chose you; we don't get the chance. You've got to go, and you've got to stay there, and you've got to be good, and you've got to be right and do whatever they want you to do and make us proud of you.' He laid the trip on me."

Count Basie took up where Walter White had left off. Lena had a chance to do something that other black women were not allowed to do: show America that a black woman could have some dignity. He renewed her sense of mission.

On returning to Hollywood, Lena learned that principal pho-
tography was scheduled to begin at last on *Cabin in the Sky,* and
she looked forward to taking on a real speaking part, instead of
doing a vaudeville act that had no relation to the film's plot line.
She did not, however, look forward to working with Ethel Waters;
for she had heard through the Hollywood grapevine that Waters
wasn't an easy person to work with.

The story line of *Cabin in the Sky* was an allegory of the
struggle between good and evil, very much in the Faust tradition.
Little Joe Jackson, the major character, gets wounded in a dice
game and, while lingering between life and death, dreams that his
soul is scheduled to go to Hell. But an angel called "The General"
appears in the dream, and he arranges for Joe to have six months
in which to atone for his sins. Joe recovers from his injuries and,
powerfully influenced by his dream, decides to mend his ways. He
is kind to his long-suffering wife, Petunia, gets a job, and only
occasionally misses his former sporting companions. But Lucifer
has already claimed his soul, and he makes it his business to cause
Joe to go astray. He arranges for Joe to win on a sweepstakes ticket
and sends a cohort, the seductress Georgia Brown, to tempt him
further. The long-suffering Petunia has been able to take just
about every other vice of Joe's, but she draws the line on Georgia
and throws him out. Unfortunately, Joe isn't very interested in
getting back into her good graces. So Petunia dresses up and goes
to Joe's hangout determined to beat Georgia at her own game.
While they are both in Jim Henry's café, a gunfight breaks out,
and both Joe and Petunia are shot. The General, upset because
Lucifer seems to have won the battle for Joe's soul, sends a tornado
to wreck the café and everyone in it. Petunia pleads with The
General and somehow manages to get them both into Heaven. All
the ruckus awakens Little Joe Jackson from his dream, and of
course the ending is a happy one, with Joe deciding, on the basis
of his dream, to reform and spend the rest of his life appreciating
Petunia.

The Broadway version, which ran for six months in 1940,
concentrated on black stereotypes and cheap humor à la *Green*

Pastures, the patronizing but highly successful play of the 1920s that was made into a movie in 1936. *Cabin in the Sky* had starred Dooley Wilson as Little Joe Jackson, Ethel Waters as Petunia, and Katherine Dunham as the temptress Georgia Brown. Naturally, the play featured a number of dance segments, compliments of Dunham and her troupe. The songs, written by Vernon Duke and John LaTouche, and Ted Fetter, were especially memorable and included the title song "Cabin in the Sky" and "Taking a Chance on Love."

MGM planned the film version to retain the basic, popular elements and to improve upon the production numbers. The result was a classic, slick MGM feature musical. Dooley Wilson was passed over in favor of Eddie "Rochester" Anderson, Lena Horne took the role that Katherine Dunham had played on Broadway, and a host of other well-known musical talents were brought in, among them Louis Armstrong, Buck and Bubbles (the famous black dance team of Ford Washington and John Sublett), and the Duke Ellington Orchestra, all of whom were nationally known. Composer Harold Arlen and lyricist Yip Harburg were called in to write new songs, and "Happiness Is Just a Thing Called Joe" would become a classic.

Some of the most obvious stereotypes were toned down. The line "eating fried chicken all the time" was deleted from the title song, and in the brawl scenes at Jim Henry's café, the razors that were de rigueur in black movies were not among the props. Filming a story in which middle-aged people were worthy of interest was in itself a minor breakthrough in the youth-oriented world of the Hollywood film studios. And, based on the foreword to the film, the thought had at least occurred to people at MGM that the conflict between good and evil just might be cross-cultural: "The folklore of America has origins in all races, all colors," the foreword solemnly stated. "This story . . . seeks to capture these values." No doubt Arthur Freed, the producer, and Vincente Minnelli, who had also directed the Broadway version, saw the movie version of *Cabin in the Sky* as forward-looking and liberal for the time, as softening the traditional stereotypes while still being marketable, and no doubt they were right.

Lena had little control over such matters. She felt it was a victory even to have been cast in a speaking role. She made a point of proving herself worthy of the opportunity. She quickly gained the respect of the film crew and the makeup and costume people for her punctuality and preparedness and for not behaving like a "temperamental star." Unfortunately, her behavior served to throw into stark relief the very temperamental behavior of Ethel Waters, who'd had a hard time climbing up the ladder of success, who intended to enjoy all the perquisites that accompanied success, and who felt not a little resentment at Lena for having it so easy.

Fortunately, the *Cabin* script called for very few scenes in which Petunia and Georgia appeared together, and that was fine with Ethel and Lena. Lena made a point of not being anywhere near Ethel at other times. But during the filming of one scene where they did appear together, Lena injured her foot, and Ethel didn't like the way everyone rushed to the aid of her young and very beautiful costar. When someone offered Lena a pillow on which to rest her cast, Ethel threw a tantrum, and the production was shut down for a day. Thereafter, the two women refused even to speak to one another.

There were other unpleasant incidents. Forty years later, Lena would recall one she had resented particularly. On the first day of shooting, when members of the *Cabin* cast went to the MGM commissary for lunch, they were met at the door by Frances Edwards, the woman who ran the commissary. She was under orders, Edwards explained, not to let the black performers into the main dining room; if they wanted to eat, they would have to eat at the counter. Samuel Marx remembers that Louis B. Mayer had no inkling of such an order and that he was surprised when he approached the commissary and found a group of black performers protesting their being barred from the main dining room. Marx, who was then a producer at MGM, wrote to the *Los*

Angeles Times in December 1982 to elaborate on Lena's recollection of the incident in a *Times* interview not long before. According to Marx, Mayer walked over to the group of angry black stars, introduced himself, and "asked if they would honor him as his guests in his private dining room. During the meal, he promised there would be no table problems thereafter, and there weren't. Lena roars like a lioness. . . . It's doubtful, though, if her roar compares to the leonine roar that Mayer was capable of making. He roared plenty loud at the executive who sent down that original order, who by the way, was L.B.'s brother."

Praise for Louis B. Mayer. But why was a major Hollywood studio, with a major all-black film in the works, segregating the stars of that film in the studio commissary? The incident did not speak well for MGM's commitment to *Cabin* or to black actors and actresses. If not for Arthur Freed and Vincente Minnelli, *Cabin* probably would not have been made and would not now be considered a classic among early black feature films.

Lena did as much as she could with the role of Georgia Brown. Georgia was supposed to be the embodiment of evil, the sensual handmaiden of Lucifer, the siren who called good men to their destruction. As played by Lena, Georgia was not evil, but naughty, more impish than destructive. How much of this image was due to Lena's acting abilities and how much was due to her fresh-faced youth and her dazzling smile is a question. Undoubtedly, she infused the role with as much dignity as she could muster and managed to be the most aloof "bad girl" ever seen in a film to date. She was not believable as a slut, and as such she was an enigmatic character who invited puzzled contemplation as much as sexual desire in the male members of audiences. When *Cabin* was released in early 1943, Lena, as much if not more than anyone else in the cast, caused critics to appreciate the underlying humor in the story. Wrote one reviewer, "There is Lena Horne as the seductive Georgia Brown, very sleek and naughty, who sings a duet with 'Rochester' called 'Life's Full of Consequences,' which is a panic." Critic Edwin Schallert spoke of her "allure" as being "one both of voice and personality." When the movie premiered at the Capitol Theater in New York, the lines waiting to get in were so long that even the usually cool and detached Duke Ellington was moved. *Cabin in the Sky* was worth waiting for. It served to lighten the spirits of a lot of moviegoers who were worried about the deepening war in Europe and the Pacific. Billed as "MGM's happy hit," guaranteed to "brighten up and cheer up" audiences, it established Lena as a star and furthered her image as one of the most enigmatic actresses in Hollywood. Somehow, in a movie that was supposed to be a comedy, and in a role that she had taken seriously, she managed to convey the impression that she was standing back and completely above it all.

6

STORMY WEATHER

NOT long after she finished filming *Cabin in the Sky,* Lena had an opportunity to return to New York. The Savoy-Plaza Hotel had invited her to perform there, the first black entertainer ever asked to play its celebrated Café Lounge. So Lena spent New Year's Eve 1942 in New York with her friends.

Lena's tenure at Café Society Downtown had led to the invitation from the Savoy-Plaza. Ivan Black, who did publicity for Café Society, had persuaded Dick Dorso, who booked acts into the Savoy-Plaza, to give her a try. Dorso naturally thought she would be grateful for the opportunity and not present much of a problem. But Lena insisted on bringing along her own accompanist. Having heard through the music-world grapevine that she would not be happy with the style of the regular pianist at the hotel, she chose Phil Moore, who had worked as her accompanist in *Panama Hattie.*

Arriving at the Savoy-Plaza, Lena learned that while the hotel had agreed to grant her wishes for professional comfort, the managers would not allow her to stay there as a guest. A room was provided in which she could change and rest between shows, but she could not sleep there. Realizing that it was important for her to play the hotel and, hopefully, open doors for other blacks, Lena chose not to protest this policy and took a room at the Theresa. Thereafter, each evening when she finished performing she swept out of the Savoy-Plaza, head held high, and went uptown to sleep. One night she became ill and fainted during her performance. The hotel managers, feeling a little ashamed of denying her accommodations, offered to call a doctor and let her stay in the hotel that night. But Lena would not give them the satisfaction of atoning for their error. Still feeling faint, she asked to be helped into a cab, which drove her to the Theresa; she called a doctor to attend her there.

Lena at the Savoy-Plaza received rave notices, and she broke even Hildegarde's attendance record. *Time, Life,* and *Newsweek* featured her in their January 4, 1943, issues. According to *Life,* in an article titled "Lena Horne: Young Negro with haunting voice charms New York with old songs," "Lena makes old song favorites sound new and exciting." The article went on to illustrate this point with a photo spread—a page full of frames showing each of Lena's gestures as she sang Cole Porter's "Let's Do It," each photo captioned by one of the phrases from the song.

Elsa Maxwell, a good friend of Porter's, sniffed in 1943, "She has every dada dodo gaga. She is a honeypot for the bees . . . but as an artist, Lena has one great fault: the fault of the cultured introvert. She hasn't the ability to project beyond herself." (Lena would later admit that Maxwell was right.) Others believed that Lena could become a highly successful cabaret singer. But Count Basie had given her a renewed sense of mission. Much as she hated to leave New York, she returned to Hollywood when her engagement at the Savoy-Plaza was over. Says Lena, "I went back out there because Basie told me that we don't usually get the chance and when we get it we have to take it. Everytime I see him, I say, 'Do you know what you did to me?'"

At the end of her month-long stint at the Savoy-Plaza, Lena returned to Los Angeles to resume her movie career with another role as a sultry chanteuse draped around a pillar. The only saving grace was that the picture was an all-black musical called *I Dood It*, starring Dooley Wilson. MGM aspired to no pretensions with this film—it was simply a fun, music-packed movie that showcased the talents of Wilson. His popularity had soared as the piano player in *Casablanca*, starring Humphrey Bogart and Ingrid Bergman, which had been released in 1942. This film was also directed by Vincente Minnelli, who apparently had been annointed by MGM as the resident director of extravaganzas and as the director who worked best with blacks. Lena was just one of several Negro stars who were cast in *I Dood It* to give it some musical excitement.

She was to do a big, complicated musical number with Hazel Scott, the pianist and singer whom she had met in New York through Barney Josephson. (At that time, Hazel was performing at Café Society Uptown, a white enclave where Lena feared to tread and where she performed only on the no-nonsense orders of Josephson when he needed a replacement performer.) The number was so complicated, in fact, that she and Hazel were scheduled to rehearse it long before it was to be recorded for the film's sound track, and longer still before they were to be photographed by the cameras.

Lena and Hazel Scott enjoyed renewing their friendship. They also enjoyed singing together under the direction of MGM vocal coach, Kay Thompson; but they didn't enjoy practicing with the conductor who was handling the musical arrangements for their number. He piddled around, changing this or that, and never seemed able to express his ideas concretely enough so that Lena, Hazel, or Kay could produce what he wanted. On more than one occasion, Kay Thompson confided to Lena and Hazel that she wished Lennie Hayton had done the arrangements.

Lena knew of Lennie Hayton. He was an arranger-in-residence at MGM and she had seen him around. But her impression of him had been negative—largely because, it seemed to her, his impression of her was negative. She didn't need to focus on yet another racist white man who averted his eyes when she passed by. She was not influenced by Kay Thompson's obvious respect for Hayton as an arranger; she merely wondered why Kay thought so well of him. When the conductor finally pronounced the Scott/Horne number worthy of a film sound track, Lena was feeling more than a little nostalgic for the musicians with whom she'd worked before she became a big Hollywood star.

As soon as she finished recording the production number for *I Dood It*, Lena went over to Twentieth Century-Fox, on "loan" from MGM, to star in Fox's latest attempt to produce an all-black musical that would have mass-audience appeal. The Fox picture was *Stormy Weather*, and it boasted the expected galaxy of black stars, among them Bill "Bojangles" Robinson, Cab Calloway and his Orchestra, the Nicholas Brothers, Katherine Dunham and her troupe, Fats Waller, a former singer at the Cotton Club named Ada Brown, and Dooley Wilson.

The plot was a thinly disguised biography of Bill Robinson, following his career almost exactly. The romantic angle involved his love for a fellow entertainer and their problems in maintaining both their romance and their careers. Largely a series of musical numbers and entertainment sketches, the film told the story of Lena and Robinson's falling in love, breaking up, and reuniting for the show's finale.

By this time, Bill Robinson was past his peak as a dancer, but he still maintained his patented grace and style. Lena's role as the sophisticated and successful singer was perfect for her except when she was called upon to sing with true emotion. Then, her aloofness and enigmatic quality were not appropriate. She needed to be more real. It was particularly important for her to sing the title song, "Stormy Weather," with genuine emotion, for she sang it following her breakup with Robinson, when she was supposed to be heartbroken. At first, the film's director, Andrew Stone, could not seem to pull the necessary feeling from her. As he told Frank Nugent of *Liberty* magazine two years later, "Lena sang it all right, but there was no warmth, no emotional quality. I did everything I could to break her down. I spoke to her about her mother, her kids. No go. Well, we shot it, but when I saw the rushes I knew it was bad. No emotions. So the next day I tried again, tried for hours, still getting nowhere. Then Cab came over. 'What's the matter?' he asked. I told him. He said, 'Leave it to me.' He walked up to Lena, whispered two words in her ear. Just two words! I never saw such a change in a person. She was wonderful! Real tears in her eyes, a sob in her voice. When she finished the number, she had hysterics, cried for ten minutes. Naturally I asked Cab what he had said. He wouldn't tell me. I still don't know."

According to Lena, Calloway said a few more words than two to her, but not many more. All it took to upset her was his mention of her own marital problems—she was in the process of obtaining a divorce from Louis—and he called her a few dirty names.

More than *Cabin in the Sky*, which was by far the better film, *Stormy Weather* and her rendition of the title song established Lena as a star. She has sung the song thousands of times since then, and forty years later it is still the song for which she receives the most frequent requests. The film itself was very successful at the box office. According to Donald Bogle, author of *Toms, Coons, Mulattoes, Mammies, and Bucks*, "The film represented wartime escapist entertainment at its peak." It was a large, expensive movie with a big production number about every five minutes and the slickest costuming and makeup Hollywood had yet seen in a black film. (Curiously, all the actresses, including Lena Horne, had to wear wigs because, according to Juliette Dandridge Ball, who worked in the film, the director said, "The only thing the colored girls need to be more beautiful is more hair." One wonders, however, if the real reason was that the hairdressers at Fox were reluctant to work on blacks' hair.) Except for Lena's rendition of "Stormy Weather," the film didn't pretend to depth. It was lively and happy, and it was greeted enthusiastically by the audiences in the all-black movie houses and by the black soldiers at segregated army camps.

Joe Louis had enlisted in the army by the time *Stormy Weather* went into production While Lena was filming the picture, he was in Hollywood to film *This Is the Army*, having arranged with the service to be stationed near Hollywood. Lena and Joe renewed the friendship that had begun in New York. Louis was married and had just recently become a father, but as he recalled in his auto-biography, "I was so carried away with her it wasn't proper. . . . I really felt I was in love with Lena, but I was feeling like a dog. I wanted to marry Lena, didn't want to leave Marva, especially now with my new baby."

According to Louis, Lena was more than a little interested in him and had been for years. Back in New York, she'd given him a gold identification bracelet with "Joe Louis" inscribed on the front and "Lena" on the back. In Hollywood, she invited him frequently to the *Stormy Weather* set and was jealous when he accepted invitations from Lana Turner to visit *her* set. Louis recalls that his relationship with Lena ended when she backed out of an agreement to keep score for Louis at a golf tournament to benefit the USO. He went to her home to have it out with her, they argued, and he returned the identification bracelet. She began to curse at him, and he hit her with a left hook. Then he began to choke her. Luckily, cousin Edwina intervened.

Lena disputes Louis's recollection of hitting or choking her, suggesting that Louis was manipulated into enlivening his memoirs. She maintains that he was her closest friend on the coast during that period, nothing more.

After Lena finished shooting *Stormy Weather* for Twentieth Century-Fox, she returned to MGM to shoot the production number in *I Dood It* for which she and Hazel Scott had earlier recorded the sound track. Vincente Minnelli was the director of the film, and Lena, who had become close friends with Minnelli, often inviting him over for dinner or going to his house for dinner, enjoyed the opportunity to work with him again. At lunchtime, they and Hazel Scott and a few other "transplanted New Yorkers" would go to the MGM commissary together. One day, Lennie Hayton walked into the commissary and joined the group. Lena said in her autobiography, *Lena*, "I guess it would be fair to say that we really saw each other for the first time. . . . It was like the recognition scene in the movies, when the boy and girl, in a blinding flash, realize that they like each other after all."

That afternoon, Lennie appeared on the set of *I Dood It* to watch Lena work. They finished shooting the number the next day, and a group of the people who had worked on it went across the street from the Culver City studios to celebrate at Frances Edwards's restaurant. Lennie showed up there and joined the party. He sat down at the piano and began to play, and Hazel and Lena sang. Lena, impressed by Lennie's extensive repertoire, was astonished to hear "Stardust" in the same arrangement as on her favorite Artie Shaw recording of the song, and impressed that Lennie had been the arranger for the recording. Hours later, everyone else in the party had gone, but Lena and Lennie stayed, playing and singing and talking about music.

Leonard George Hayton, who had been married once before and who, like Louis Jones, was nine years Lena's senior, had grown up on Manhattan's Lower East Side. In the 1920s he'd played piano with Bix Biederbecke, Red Nicholas, and Paul Whiteman, among others. From there he'd gone on to form his own band, and in the late 1920s-early 1930s he and his band were featured performers on the radio show "Lucky Strike Hit Parade." In 1932 he went with Bing Crosby to California where he accompanied Crosby in *The Big Broadcast* and did the arrangement for Crosby's recording of "Please." He'd joined MGM as a composer-conductor in 1941 and did many pictures with that studio, among them *The Harvey Girls* with Judy Garland and *Singin' in the Rain* with Gene Kelly.

Lennie Hayton lived and breathed music, and with him Lena experienced the artistic rapport that she felt with Billy Strayhorn and Teddy Wilson. "First of all," she later recalled, "he played music for me—every kind. I hadn't known any classical music since my grandfather died, and I was too little then to know what it was. Lennie played all sorts of music, and he explained it structurally and architecturally. I was beginning to be a little brighter and I could understand. He knew the way to teach me

87

what I needed to know. He laid the cushion down, which all fine musicians do, and you don't have to worry about anything but what you do."

It was just as well that Lena began again to concentrate on her singing, for the next movie roles she was given allowed her little opportunity to develop her acting skills. She would later consider herself lucky to have appeared in *Cabin in the Sky* and *Stormy Weather*, with their comparatively meaty roles. Had she arrived in Hollywood much earlier, or much later, in the 1940s, she might not have had the opportunity to appear in a major all-black film.

An article in *The New York Times* in February 1943 shed some light on the increase in all-black films at that time. The article read in part: "Two major studios, Metro-Goldwyn-Mayer and Twentieth Century-Fox, in producing pictures with all-Negro casts, are following the desires of Washington in making such films at this time. Decisions to produce the pictures, it is stated, followed official expression that the Administration felt that its program for increased employment of Negro citizens in certain heretofore restricted fields of industry would be helped by a general distribution of important pictures in which Negroes played a major part."

But in producing major all-black films like *Cabin* and *Stormy Weather*, the two studios no doubt felt that they had done their duty. The parts Lena was subsequently offered were more parts as a "pillar singer" in predominantly white movies, among them *Swing Fever*, released in 1943, and *Broadway Rhythm* and *Two Girls and a Sailor*, both released in 1944. Typical of her billing was the cast list of *Two Girls and a Sailor*, which starred June Allyson, Gloria De Haven, and Van Johnson:

CAST

Patsy Deyo .... June Allyson
Jean Deyo .... Gloria De Haven
John Dyckman Brown III .... Van Johnson
....
Specialty [#16 in a list of 19] .... Lena Horne

In 1944 she was part of a "galaxy" of stars in *Ziegfeld Follies*. *Variety*, in its August 14, 1945, review, called her appearance "outstanding . . . showing the gal can act as well as sing and posture," but she was given no more opportunities to act in 1944.

Nineteen forty-four was a particularly rough year for Lena. As she began to spend more time with Lennie Hayton, cousin Edwina became more disapproving. Lena didn't often have Lennie to her house, feeling that her children would be confused; but Edwina knew from Lena's manner that she was seeing a lot of Lennie. Edwina held firmly to the age-old black women's belief that white men use black women. While Lena acknowledged that this belief was firmly rooted in historical fact, she knew that Lennie was not a user; but she couldn't convince her cousin. At length, Edwina gave Lena an ultimatum: either she stop seeing Lennie or Edwina was leaving. Lena, after considerable thought, chose Lennie. She didn't like breaking with a family member, and she didn't know what she was going to do about Gail and Teddy; but she cared too much about Lennie and about her own independence to give in to her cousin's pressure. Fortunately, Lena met a woman whose husband was serving in the army and who was alone with her child; and Mrs. Ida Starks and her daughter came to live with Lena and her children.

Not long after Mrs. Starks and her daughter moved in with her and Teddy and Gail, Lena was forced to confront a problem she knew would surface eventually: the endemic racism of Hollywood aimed at her children. While she had managed to come to terms with that racism as directed against her, she could not allow it to affect her children. When Gail and Teddy and Mrs. Starks's daughter came home from school one day to report that their classmates had called them "nigger," Lena felt as if her heart would burst open. Quickly turning her pain into rage, she went to the school to have the matter out with Gail's teacher. But the teacher professed to be powerless against the already-ingrained racism of the young "Okie" and "Arkie" children who predominated in the school's population, and Lena realized there was no way to protect her children in Hollywood short of hiring a private tutor. At length, she decided to relocate her family in New York and, through the help of Cab Calloway, found a house in a racially integrated neighborhood in St. Albans, Queens. She kept the house on Horn Avenue and commuted between Hollywood and New York.

Lena and Louis were divorced in 1944, and Lena lost custody of Teddy, which she had enjoyed informally for several months between the time Louis and their son had arrived in Hollywood and the time she decided to move her family back East. Louis had been eager to assume the management of Lena's career in Hollywood, and she later felt that she lost the opportunity to gain formal custody of Teddy by turning Louis down. She agreed that Louis was clever and ambitious, but she knew that one needed more than those qualities to be a successful agent in Hollywood. One needed connections, and a reputation, and most of all, one needed to be white. Louis knew nothing about playing the Hollywood games, and Lena was afraid that having Louis as her agent would be worse than having no agent at all—he might do serious damage to her career. Although she tried to explain the logic of her reasoning to her husband, Louis refused to understand. Arrangements for their divorce proceeded quite quickly after that.

To this day, Lena regrets not having put up more of a fight for custody of Teddy. But her agents and attorneys assured her that the resulting publicity would hurt her. She would be portrayed by Louis's attorneys, and in the press, as a selfish woman who had put her career ahead of her concern for the welfare of her children. There was even the possibility that if the mudslinging that would inevitably result became too extreme, she might jeopardize the arrangement by which she had custody of Gail. She didn't fight for Teddy, and thus she deprived both him and herself of the normal parent-child relationship she had wanted so much to enjoy with her children.

Louis left California, taking Teddy with him, and took a job as advertising manager of the *Cleveland Gazette,* a black newspaper. Lena did receive part-time custody of her son, and at various agreed-upon times he visited her. He was too young to understand the legal arrangements worked out between his parents and their respective attorneys, but he seemed to enjoy commanding the attention of first one parent and then the other. He was old enough to know that his mother was a famous person, and when he visited Lena he liked to let everyone else know it, too. When they rode in a cab, which was often because Lena didn't know how to drive, he banged on the partition to get the driver's attention and yelled, "I betcha don't know my mother's a movie star, I betcha!" After a while, however, he became aware that his time with his mother would take the form of visits only, and he would not understand for many years why and how the custody situation had come about.

During the time when the details of her divorce from Louis were being worked out, Lena came to rely on Lennie more than ever. He was quiet and supportive, didn't offer her advice unless she asked for it, and only then if he felt it was proper for him to give advice. He urged her to concentrate on her music, and she found great release in putting her troubles into the songs she sang. They tried to conduct their relationship as discreetly as possible, rarely appearing together in public during nonworking hours, preferring to meet at Lennie's or at the homes of trusted friends. At times, Lena wondered how the relationship could go anywhere, given the social climate of the country; but while she was going through so many problems and so much pain she preferred not to think about the future. She only knew that she needed Lennie very much.

During 1944, with so little studio work to occupy her, Lena spent a great deal of time entertaining U.S. troops in various parts of the country. Lena had gotten involved in community activities very soon after her arrival in Hollywood. She had joined the local chapter of the NAACP and HICCASP (Hollywood Independent Citizens Committee of the Arts, Sciences, and Professions), a group that promoted various liberal causes; she had also worked with Assemblyman Gus Hawkins to promote a Fair Employment Practices Commission in California. When Hollywood committed itself to supporting the war effort, not only turning out patriotic movies but also providing in-person entertainment at USO clubs and various military bases around the country, Lena was an eager participant—and not just when it was convenient.

At Christmastime, 1943, several scheduled entertainers had canceled their appearances at the Hollywood Canteen. The situation became particularly acute on Christmas day. Lena was in the midst of planning a party when the program director of the Canteen called to ask, apologetically, if she could appear on short notice. She'd been singing at the Canteen once a week for months, but her only question was, "Are you sure the boys aren't tired of me?" Assured that they were not, she dressed hurriedly and arrived at the Canteen barely half an hour later. Hours after that, having brightened the Christmas of hundreds of soldiers, she returned to what was left of her own Christmas party.

With the release of *Cabin in the Sky* and *Stormy Weather* in 1943, Lena had quickly become the favorite star of blacks in the military and their No. 1 pinup girl. She never gave much credence to that distinction, being aware that she was just about the only pinup girl available to the black troops, who would have gotten into serious trouble if anyone had found a picture of Hedy Lamarr or Betty Grable in their possession. There were 800,000 black soldiers and one Lena, and they named their planes, their jeeps, even the roads they built, after her. In 1945, there was a "Lena Horne Lane" on an Italian mountainside, a road that led to the camp of the 332nd Fighter Group, composed of four black pursuit squadrons. Although black soldiers weren't alone in having crushes on Lena—plenty of white soldiers wrote to her for pictures—and while Lena was eager to perform for the men who were defending her country, regardless of their race, she couldn't help resenting the treatment of the black soldiers she encountered.

In 1944 the army asked her to do a camp tour of the South, and she found that everywhere she went there was strict segregation of the black troops. She would sing in a fairly well-appointed auditorium to an all-white group of soldiers, then be escorted to a shacklike mess hall, in which a makeshift stage had been hastily erected, to entertain the black troops. On the bases where black and white troops were allowed to sit in the same auditorium, the black troops always had to sit in the back.

Traveling in the South was not exactly pleasant for Lena, even though she was doing it for a patriotic cause. On occasion, she suffered discrimination equal to that which the black troops endured. One February, the army arranged for her to attend the graduation exercises at the Tuskegee Flying School, where the men of the all-black 99th Pursuit Squadron, which later became so famous, were trained. Her plane schedule involved a half-hour layover at an Alabama airport before she took a connecting flight to Tuskegee, and during that time (it was 3:00 A.M.), she wanted a cup of coffee. Fully aware of Southern social patterns, she first asked a terminal hostess if she could go in to the lunch counter. The hostess, perhaps recognizing her, said it would be all right. Lena entered the lunchroom, sat down at the counter, and watched the waitress pass by several times without appearing to notice her. When at last the waitress asked what she wanted and Lena told her, the waitress said she couldn't serve her. After Lena explained that a terminal hostess had told her that it would be all right, the waitress said, "Well, if you'll go around back to the kitchen, I'll see what I can do." Lena told her not to bother. Just then, a teenage boy, who had been washing dishes, looked up and asked, "Aren't you Lena Horne?" Lena said she was. His eyes lit up immediately, and he shoved a greasy menu across the counter, saying, "Would you autograph it, please?" Lena signed the menu and walked out of the lunchroom, without having had the cup of coffee.

At Tuskegee, Colonel Noel Parish, the white commanding officer who escorted her to the graduation dinner, presented her to the cadets as evidence that "the charm and beauty of womanhood are not confined to any one race."

Lena endured many such painful ironies as she traveled in the South entertaining American troops, but she told herself she could take them. After all, she was working for an important cause, and she had few illusions about what it was like in the South for blacks. But, on one occasion, she simply could not remain quiet in the face of obvious racism any longer: that was when she found herself expected to entertain in a black mess hall in which German prisoners of war were seated in front of the black soldiers. That flew in the face of her patriotism, and she protested, loudly. She went to the local NAACP office and complained, and she complained, too, to the Hollywood sponsors of her Southern USO tour. In response, the sponsoring organizations refused to pay her for further appearances in Southern camps. Henceforth, when she was specifically invited to entertain black troops at a Southern camp, Lena paid her own expenses.

Back in Hollywood, and undaunted, Lena went to work on behalf of Japanese-American soldiers who had been wounded fighting for the United States; they'd returned home to find that they couldn't get adequate housing and they faced discrimination similar to that suffered by other Californians of Japanese heritage. Her activism and her comparative lack of reluctance to speak out against discrimination earned her a lot of sideways looks from both blacks and whites. But Lena was a big enough star to use her fame for good purposes, and at the same time she would not be made to suffer unduly for it. By today's standards, her attempts seem relatively cautious, but America in the 1940s was a different place.

In November 1944, Lena was booked into the all-black Howard Theater in Washington, DC. Since MGM had no parts to offer her, Lena's agents had persuaded the studio to allow her to take singing engagements. The Howard show was one to which Lena particularly looked forward, and she arrived several days early to appear at press parties. As the Washington, DC, representative for the National Negro Press Association (NNPA) reported, Lena proved to be:

> a worthy ambassador of good will and better race relations for the Negro. . . . This correspondent was amazed at the fluent manner

in which she intelligently discussed unions, politics, race relations, social welfare. . . . But here's an actual development for which Lena Horne may be given credit. At the press party were representatives of the local white press—theater critics and even editors. No other person, very likely, could have drawn them there despite the cordial invitation extended. Most of them had never come in contact with members of the Negro press before—or with any intelligent Negroes, for that matter. A few of them were so impressed that plans are under way now for an interracial press luncheon so more of the "white" press may learn what goes on.

While the NNPA correspondent was accurate in believing that Lena Horne was the one black entertainer who could draw the white press to a publicity party, he may have been operating under the assumption that Lena had had some say in who was invited. If so, he probably was wrong. Lena was still sufficiently naïve, or sufficiently otherwise engaged, not to pay much attention to what her agents were doing. She'd occasionally been very unhappy with the way they had handled her publicity and her career, but she saw no reason to change from one white agent to another. What happened with the Howard Theater engagement caused her to pay more attention to what her management was doing.

Given all the preengagement publicity, Lena expected to sing to a packed house, and when, on opening night, she performed before a sparse audience, she believed, at first, that perhaps she had become a person with whom ordinary blacks could not identify. She was keenly aware that she was open to charges of selling out, despite her USO tours and her membership in liberal organizations, by virtue of having achieved comparative success. But she was in Washington, DC, and she knew that the black community there was a large and varied one and capable of producing a sizable audience for her. She decided to investigate the reasons behind the nearly empty house.

She found out that her agents had arranged to charge exorbitant ticket prices—higher even than those for Ella Fitzgerald when she performed at the Howard. They were prices similar to those charged at high-class white clubs. Blacks in Washington, DC, had stayed away because most of them couldn't afford the tickets, and those who could naturally suspected that she had committed the unforgivable sin of trying to be like white folks.

Lena took immediate action. She called her managers in California and threatened to cancel her engagement at the Howard if they didn't agree to a lowering of ticket prices. Once this was done, she called upon the manager of the Howard Theater to appear with her at a special press conference at which she announced new, lower ticket prices and explained that she'd had no idea that such high prices were charged initially. The press, both black and white, dutifully spread the word, and Lena's engagement at the Howard ended on a note of success. Once word got around that tickets were available at a reasonable rate, Lena had her packed house, night after night.

7

TROUBLE IN HOLLYWOOD

LENA did a great deal of club and radio work in the mid-1940s. In the fall of 1944 she did a program for the "Suspense" radio series titled "You Were Wonderful" and received a flood of mail from listeners. She was a regular on "Jubilee," the all-Negro army radio broadcast and frequently sang on "Command Performance," the army's radio show. She was a favorite pinup girl and especially popular with her male audiences. Frances Williams recalls, "She was breaking every man's heart who was near her or who had even heard about her. I remember I was working in Palm Springs and I was out by the pool. All these men were playing gin rummy, and someone said something about Lena Horne. Well, after that there was no gin rummy. You couldn't get near a telephone. They were all on the phones trying to find *some* woman to come down to Palm Springs. They had been ignited. That's what she did to men at that time."

Lena took it all in stride. "I looked exactly like everybody else in Hollywood except I was a bronze one. They weren't interested in *me*. I had one man say to me, 'You know I fantasize about you . . .

you're like a Polynesian, long black hair.' I said, 'It isn't me.' I never got carried away."

But the letters they wrote were addressed to Lena Horne. At Metro-Goldwyn-Mayer, according to Frank Nugent, a reporter for *Liberty* magazine, Lena's movie fan mail stacked up with June Allyson's and Walter Pidgeon's, even though she had had exactly one major role in an MGM picture. By the spring of 1945 she decided she needed help with her correspondence. "I never thought I'd need a secretary," she told Nugent, "but this is getting beyond me. Of course it's wonderful the way they write. Some of the letters just break me up. You can't turn letters like that over to the fan-mail department. They're not fan letters. They're—well, they're letters you have to sit down and answer yourself."

She was the nation's top black entertainer and, by the standards of the day, well paid. MGM paid her $1,000 a week for forty weeks a year. Her fees for theater and nightclub appearances were $6,500 a week plus a percentage of the gate, which could sometimes add up to $3,500 or more. She received $1,500 to $2,500 for her radio shows, and she was getting royalties on her earlier recordings as well as on her more recent MGM singles—"Smoochie," "Take Love Easy," "He Makes Me Believe He's Mine"—and albums—*Little Girl Blue, Classics in Blue.*

The fact that she was maintaining households on both coasts, paying musicians to accompany her on road tours, and paying the salary of a secretary went unrecognized by many, among them the woman who believed that she was responsible for Lena's success. Lena's mother had showed up in Hollywood not long before Lena had moved her family back East. Reading fan magazines in Cuba had given Edna Rodriguez the impression that Lena was a big star, and Edna didn't believe Lena was sending her and Mike enough money. Edna also had the idea that Lena was close to lots of major producers and could help her get work in the movies. When Lena insisted that she didn't have these important connections, Edna went to her daughter's home when Lena was away and demanded Lena's address book from Mrs. Starks. Edna wouldn't believe that Lena couldn't help her and when all else failed, she threatened to go to the newspapers with stories about what an ungrateful daughter Lena had been. Eventually, Lena had to work out an agreement, through an attorney, under which she would send more money to her mother if her mother didn't go public with her resentments.

During the time she was in Los Angeles, Edna stayed in a downtown white hotel; having managed to avoid the sharp-eyed desk clerks' suspicions, she passed for white. When Lena wanted to see her mother she had to send Lennie into the hotel to ask for her, since Lena Horne, big star, would not have been welcome in the hotel and would have blown her mother's cover by visiting her in person.

Even in the comparatively rarified atmosphere of the movie world, Lena had to contend with white hostility or, at the other extreme, white exploitation. Most Hollywood blacks had not forgiven her for challenging the established system of role getting, and she still faced social ostracism from them. Her circle of friends was comparatively small. Among whites, it included MGM producer Arthur Freed; another MGM producer, Fred Finkelhoffe and his wife, singer Ella Logan; Vincente Minnelli; composer Harold Arlen; and actor Gene Kelly—almost all of these people were transplanted New Yorkers. Among blacks, there were Dorothy Dandridge, who was the next most popular black pinup girl; Katherine Dunham; Hattie McDaniel; Cab Calloway; and Billy Strayhorn. She was also close to Hazel Washington, who had once been Rosalind Russell's personal maid and who operated her own leather goods business in Hollywood. Lena had dated Hazel's nephew, Kenny, a former halfback at UCLA. Another friend who was not in the entertainment business was Elois Davis, wife of the doctor whom most of the black stars in Hollywood recommended. Her closest friend was Lennie Hayton, but Lena didn't see him as often as she would have liked, for fear of the public reaction.

Most nights found her alone—in hotel rooms when she was on the road—reading and listening to music. Under Lennie's tutelage, she had developed a liking for the music of Tchaikovsky and

Stravinsky. She had also acquired a sizable jazz collection in which clarinetists Sidney Bechet and Edwin Hall were prominent. She read murder mysteries for relaxation and biographies for instruction, and in the spring of 1945 she was reading about the life of Thomas Paine. If she had wanted, she could have been out nearly every night, for many men in Hollywood, and many Hollywood hostesses, considered her a feather in their caps; but she confined her public appearances to functions at which MGM virtually commanded her presence, such as press parties and movie previews. These she felt she had to attend, for the studio was paying her a comparatively hefty salary for very little work.

Being black continued to place her in an awkward position as a star under contract to a major movie studio. She had to contend with what former MGM producer Arthur Marx calls "the painful pragmatism of the company's sales department because, as in most industries, even today, sales take precedence over manufacturing." This "painful pragmatism" caused her to lose her speaking part in the one movie she filmed at MGM in 1945.

Till the Clouds Roll By was a musical biography of composer Jerome Kern and it was packed with stars, for there was a plethora of production numbers featuring shows on which Kern had worked. Arthur Freed produced it, and Vincent Minnelli directed it, and they asked Lena what Kern number she would like to sing in the film. Lena chose "Can't Help Lovin' That Man of Mine," a Kern song from the Broadway musical *Show Boat* and thus was cast, in the *Show Boat* sequence, as the quadroon, Julie, along with Tony Martin (Ravenal) and Kathryn Grayson (Magnolia).

The original script called for Lena, as Julie, to speak a few lines to Magnolia—words of advice, as if to a friend or a sister. The scriptwriters forgot to take into account the Southern taboo against a black talking to a white in familiar terms, but the MGM brass never forgot the "painful pragmatism" of sales. As Lena said ruefully in 1947, "I didn't say Ma'am or Missy, so naturally some higher-up cut all my speaking part." When the movie was released, Lena received excellent reviews for singing the Kern classic as it had never been sung before; but she hadn't advanced her career as an actress, having spoken no lines.

What else could she expect from a studio—or for that matter, from an industry—that depended so heavily on Southern exhibitors for its profits? The ever-vigilant Southern censors could spot a dignified portrayal of a black a mile away, even when it was couched in layers upon layers of white fluff. The best example of Southern censorship was the reception in Tennessee of *Ziegfeld Follies*, which reached that state in the summer of 1946. The stars were, in order of listing: Fred Astaire, William Powell, Lucille Ball, Lucille Bremer, Fanny Brice, Judy Garland, Kathryn Grayson, Lena Horne, Gene Kelly, James Melton, Victor Moore, Red Skelton, and Esther Williams. It featured another nine performers. But when the film reached Knoxville, Tennessee, Emil Bernstecker, the city's reigning theater magnate, cut all the scenes in which Lena appeared, since they "might prove objectionable to some people in Knoxville." Since Lena's name had been used in most advertisements of the picture, someone in Knoxville had to black out her name on all the posters. In Memphis, no formal announcement was made, but Lena's sequence was deleted from the film for all showings in the city. The correspondent for the American Negro Press wrote, "Censor Chairman Lloyd T. Binford . . . is noted for his use of the shears on any scenes involving Negroes which do not degrade them."

By 1945, studios like MGM believed that they had fulfilled their commitment to the government to provide more work for black actors; and since the government didn't seem to be pressuring them any longer they made few moves to produce more all-black shows. MGM, for one, was content to feature one or two popular black performers in its musicals, knowing full well that these segments would be deleted by Southern censors. MGM's problem was that it had Lena Horne under contract and was paying her $40,000 a year, and the studio wasn't getting much of a return on its investment. Trying to break the contract was not even considered, for Lena remained the top black entertainer, and MGM was not about to lose her to a rival studio. However, in return for its investment, the studio expected Lena to be willing to do whatever work did come along for her. The studio bosses were surprised and angry to find that Lena would have no part of this tacit agreement.

That year, 1945, Arthur Freed decided to get involved in the production of *St. Louis Woman* on Broadway. The play, based on the novel *God Sends Sunday* by black writer Arna Bontemps, had been adapted for the stage by Bontemps himself, with the help of fellow black writer Countee Cullen. Freed had gotten the famous white songwriting team of Harold Arlen and Johnny Mercer to do the score, and he wanted Lena to play the leading character. Through his solid connections with MGM, Freed had no trouble gaining the studio's consent to use Lena, in return for a fee, and when he presented Lena with the script and the score he considered her participation in the show practically a fait accompli.

Lena liked the score, especially the song "Come Rain or Come Shine." She didn't think much of the script. Set in the 1820s, it was supposed to be a story based on history; but in reality it was another thinly disguised vaudeville show, with singing and dancing breaking out all over the place. What it had to say about black jockeys—in the early 1800s there were no white jockeys—was subsumed under the gloss of happy blacks singing and dancing and to the major story about a hard-riding, fast-loving jockey and a flashy St. Louis whore. To Lena's mind, it was just another version of the same old stereotypes. Lena was getting bored with sporting-life characters; she gave the script and the score back to Freed and told him she would prefer to play a role that reflected real black life.

Freed, who fancied himself a liberal in many ways, was astonished at Lena's reaction, and the MGM bosses were equally nonplussed. Here she'd been given the chance to appear on Broadway —a golden opportunity—and she'd turned it down like some prima donna. They applied pressure, reminding her that she was under contract and was not a free agent, appealing to their idea of her sense of racial responsibility by pointing out that she could reopen Broadway to blacks. But Lena wasn't alone in feeling that the part of the St. Louis woman was degrading and that the entire script was a flagrant homage to the age-old stereotypes. Her trusted friends agreed with her assessment of the script; they urged her to remain firm in her refusal to be associated with the play, and she did.

St. Louis Woman was produced without Lena—parts for black actresses never went begging. Pearl Bailey, an up-and-coming young singer, was signed for the role, to play opposite Harold Nicholas as "Little Augie," the jockey. Rex Ingram had the role as the saloonkeeper. But the play went into rehearsals amid considerable controversy. Copies of the script had circulated around the entertainment world, and the NAACP, among other black organizations, had come out against the production for its fostering of negative racial stereotypes. Worried that this vociferous criticism would hurt the show once it opened on Broadway, the producers of the show replaced Pearl Bailey ten days before its scheduled Broadway opening. Instead, they hired Muriel Rahn, an already-established black singer who, the producers felt, would bring more interest to the play. But it was Bailey, not Rahn, who played the role of the St. Louis woman on opening night. At the last minute, Harold Nicholas and Rex Ingram staged a "wildcat strike" and refused to go onstage with Muriel Rahn. They charged that she made them feel uneasy. Perhaps they simply resented the last-minute replacement of Bailey by Rahn; perhaps the real problem was that Rahn didn't know the part well enough. Preceded by so much controversy, and beset by cast changes that caused great unrest among everyone involved, the show limped onto Broadway, where it received lukewarm reviews. Countee Cullen had died in January 1946, and the show's publicists had tried to associate the play with some sort of tribute to the late writer, but the critics resisted that obvious appeal to their sympathy.

Ed Gross, the white, primary producer of the show, stated publicly that he would never produce another Negro show, and the organizations that had been against it from the beginning felt a certain sense of victory, although they regretted the problems caused the black actors. Lena's reputation in the black community received a boost from it all. She had refused to be associated with the show from the very beginning. As the *Los Angeles Sentinel*, a black newspaper, put it:

> Five encores and three curtain calls for lovely Lena Horne for her stand on the "St. Louis Woman" deal. Not only is the play rift with backstage quarrels but the music, story, and acting came in for a panning from the critics. All of which proves that Miss Horne not only knows a derogatory play when she sees one, but also can smell a bad one, all the way from her lovely home on Horn Ave., above the Strip.

Neither Arthur Freed nor MGM ever admitted that Lena might have been right in refusing the title role in the play. What stuck in their collective craw was that she had defied them, and they had the power to retaliate in ways that would hurt her. A revival of *Show Boat* was being planned for Broadway—it opened two months before *St. Louis Woman*, at the Ziegfeld Theater in January 1946—but even though Jerome Kern specifically asked that Lena play Julie, the studio refused. Nor was Lena offered any more movie roles, not even a "pillar part," in any of the numerous musicals the studio regularly churned out. And if that were not enough, the studio became extremely reluctant to allow Lena to accept nightclub and theater engagements, except for those at Loews Theaters, where an appearance by Lena was good for MGM's business.

The enforced idleness was frustrating for Lena; even more frustrating was her inability to challenge any of the MGM bosses to come straight-out and tell her why she had been placed, as she put it, "in dry dock." She couldn't even get past the secretaries and neither could her agents. In Hollywood, rumors circulated that she had actually been fired by MGM, although the rumormongers preferred to believe that the reason was her relationship with Lennie rather than her refusal to appear in *St.*

Lena at age sixteen. The photograph was taken by writer/photographer Carl Van Vechten at Joe Louis's New Jersey training camp, where Lena's father introduced her to the heavyweight champion. (Theatre Collection, Museum of the City of New York)

A photograph of Lena that ran in the *New York Daily News* in 1934 when she was a chorus girl at the Cotton Club. The caption read: "Rhythm's her middle name. The girls who dance and sing in the Harlem hot spots haven't any use for tame music. Take Lena Horne, for example, tossing her medicine ball around on the beach of the Lido Recreation Centre. When she sings, she's got to feel the music. Same with her dancing. She wants music that's wild, that sets her afire, that runs like flame through her blood. Then she's got rhythm." (Theatre Collection, Museum of the City of New York)

Avon Long and Lena in the number "As Long as I Live," 1934. The opportunity to appear with Long was Lena's first break at the Cotton Club. *Frank Driggs Collection)*

Lena and Noble Sissle, 1936 *(Frank Driggs Collection)*

Lena, ca. 1935–1940
(Frank Driggs Collection)

Lena with Thornton Hall in *I Dood It*, 1943 (Frank Driggs
Collection)

Lena at the Savoy-Plaza in New York in 1943. It was this engagement that brought her coverage in national magazines like *Life* and catapulted her to national fame. *(Wide World Photos)*

Lena at a Progressive Citizens of America rally in 1947. At right is Paul Robeson, her long-time friend and vice chairman of the PCA. *(Wide World Photos)*

Lena in *Broadway Rhythm*, 1944, in a musical "specialty sequence" easily cut from the film when it played in Southern theaters. *(Frank Driggs Collection)*

Lena at the London Casino, spring 1947. In a few months, she and Lennie would return to Europe to be married. *(Wide World Photos)*

Lena and Lennie arriving in New York from France, September 1950 *(Wide World Photos)*

Lena shakes hands with a French locomotive engineer on arriving in Paris from New York, spring 1950. *(Wide World Photos)*

Lena and Lennie in Paris, May 1954. After they made their marriage public in 1950, they spent as much time as they could in Europe. *(Pictorial Parade)*

Lena in *Meet Me in Las Vegas*, 1956. Having refused to appear in roles that she considered undignified, Lena was offered only "specialty sequences" in a couple of films in the 1950s. *(Frank Driggs Collection)*

Lena at the Coconut Grove in New York, 1956. Lennie is conducting. *(Wide World Photos)*

Lena and her daughter, Gail, in Paris in the late 1950s. Gail once explained her designation as one of the best-dressed young women in New York by citing her mother's policy of wearing a gown herself only once, and then passing it along to Gail. *(Wide World Photos)*

Lena in *Jamaica*, which ran for over a year on Broadway in 1958–1959 (*Theatre Collection, Museum of the City of New York*)

Lena with Eleanor Roosevelt in 1960. The two women had met often in the course of their efforts on behalf of various social causes. *(Wide World Photos)*

Lena at the March on Washington, August 28, 1963 *(Pictorial Parade)*

Lena in London in 1966. Reporters made much of her "mod" look. She prefers slacks and jackets and turtleneck sweaters even today. *Pictorial Parade*)

Lena on the set of *Patch*, later retitled *Death of a Gunfighter*, 1968 (*Wide World Photos*)

Lena in 1975 (Frank Driggs Collection)

Lena and her son-in-law, Sidney Lumet, arriving at the Plaza Hotel in New York for the 1971 opening-night party for The Prisoner of Second Avenue. (Pictorial Parade)

The elegant Lena, still as beautiful as when she made her Hollywood debut, shortly after her 62nd birthday in 1979. *(Pictorial Parade)*

Lena with old friend James Mason, backstage at the Nederlander Theater in 1982. When she and Lennie went to London in 1947, Mason suggested that they get in touch with his family, and the British Masons provided them with fresh eggs—a rare commodity in London after World War II. *(Wide World Photos)*

On opening night of *Lena Horne: The Lady and Her Music*, 1981, at the Nederlander Theater on Broadway, Lena received standing ovations after each act and after two individual songs in the show. *(Wide World Photos)*

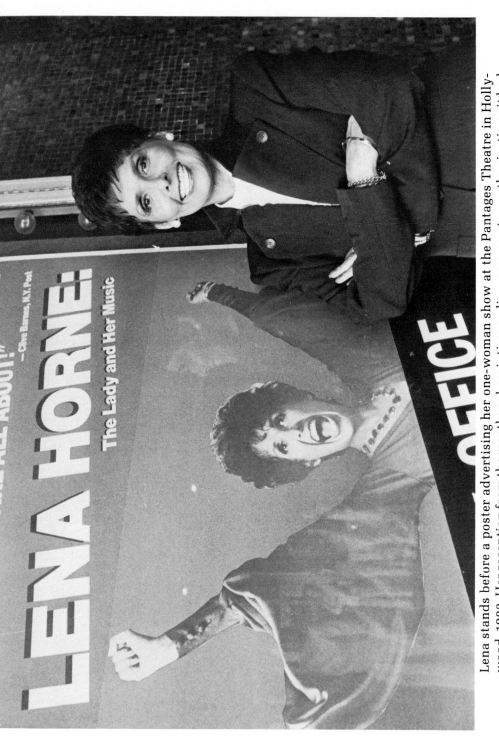

Lena stands before a poster advertising her one-woman show at the Pantages Theatre in Holly-wood, 1982. Her reception from the mostly subscription audience was not as enthusiastic as it had been in New York, but she kept on. (*Wide World Photos*)

Louis Woman. Joan Crawford heard the rumors and approached Lena at a party to give her some advice.

"Get a bigger agency to manage you," Crawford suggested. A larger and more powerful agency would be able to get past the secretaries to the men who surrounded Louis B. Mayer. Then, it could work on softening up these men so that Lena could see Mayer himself. Only Mayer could lift the embargo on Lena. Crawford knew this from experience, having been forced to go begging to Mayer once herself. Lena was hardly eager to crawl to L.B., but she realized she couldn't go on much longer under the present circumstances. She needed to make some money. She was sending money to her mother, supporting her family in Queens, and carrying the expenses of the house on Horn Avenue. She employed three musicians to travel with her on road trips; she had to pay them whether she was working or not, otherwise she'd lose them. Following the step-by-step advice that Joan Crawford had given her, she went to MCA, the largest agency in Hollywood, which took her on immediately and arranged for her to buy out her contract with the Louis Shurr agency. Then representatives of MCA went to work at getting her an appointment with L. B. Mayer, who acted pained at her ungratefulness but paternally accepted her apologies. Thereafter, while she still received no offers for movie parts, she was able to accept club dates.

One of the most important for her was an engagement at the Copacabana in New York, where she hadn't performed since her stint at the Savoy-Plaza in 1942. She was engaged at the main, upstairs room, where no black entertainer had ever performed before. She practiced hard for the engagement and on opening night was so concerned with her performance that she didn't notice the composition of the audience. But when Billie Holiday came backstage to see her, she learned that blacks weren't being admitted. Holiday was one of the few exceptions. Outside the club, blacks picketed in protest against this blatant segregation. While Lena says her first reaction was "Why me?" she soon decided to do something about the situation. She met with the club's managers but got no satisfaction from them; they pointed out that there was nothing in her contract guaranteeing that blacks would be admitted. Blacks had never tried to gain admittance to the Copa, according to the managers. Lena couldn't legally break her contract, so she did the only thing she could do: she issued a public statement that she had no knowledge of the club's policies when she had agreed to appear there and promised that henceforth she would have in all her contracts a clause that would provide for unrestricted admissions policies. According to Lena's autobiography, when she returned to the club in later years, she did not believe that blacks had been denied admission although she was never sure: "I returned there in '46 and there were certainly Negroes in the audience, but I was never absolutely certain that this was more than tokenism."

Ted Poston, writing in the *New York Post* in 1956, remembered differently. In a column titled "Jim Crow in New York," he recalled the time Lena played the Copa in 1948. Bill "Bojangles" Robinson and a "well-known Negro actress" were met at the door by a beefy doorman who refused to honor their reservations, and the actress telephoned Lena in her dressing room, upbraiding her for appearing at a club where "your people are treated like that" and promising to let the whole world know what was going on. Lena, "half hysterical," according to Poston, had called him and Major Robinson, another reporter, for advice.

Wrote Poston, "The reporters immediately set up a standard battle plan which even as recently as 1948 Negroes often had to use to obtain their civil rights in New York City." Enlisting the help of a white reporter for the *Post*, Victor Riesel, they called and made a reservation for a party of four in Poston's name. The next night, Riesel arrived half an hour before show time and said he was with "Mr. Poston's party." He was ushered in, and when Jack Entratter, manager of the Copa, saw the columnist he immediately shifted the "Poston table" to ringside and ordered a round of drinks on the house. Fifteen minutes later, Poston and his wife arrived. The doorman informed them that they had no reservation. Meanwhile, Robinson arrived with a policeman. Entratter, informed of the problem at his door, announced that no one could enter without a reservation. Just then, Riesel appeared and informed Entratter that Poston was his host. Reluctantly, Entratter instructed the doorman to let the blacks in.

Later, between shows, Entratter joined the party, which Lena had also joined, and tried to explain the fears of the downtown club owners about Negro patrons. As related by Poston:

> First, of course, was the oft-expressed fear that "customers come here from everywhere. Suppose some Southern patron came in and saw Negroes here. Anything could happen."
>
> He admitted, however, that he had never heard anything untoward happening in downtown clubs which did admit Negroes and nodded in half-agreement when he was told: "Look, no matter how loud they holler down home, when crackers come to New York, they *expect* to see Negroes in places of public accommodation. The last thing a cracker would do is pick a fight in a community where he feels himself a minority."
>
> Entratter's second fear—and apparently that of his 1948 confrères—was that if one Negro was admitted to a club, the place would be flooded with Negroes later.
>
> "Why?" he was asked. "We've never been to the Copa before nor had any desire to come here. If you hadn't kicked Bojangles and the actress around, we wouldn't be here now."

According to Poston, it was then that the Copacabana lifted its restrictions on admitting blacks who had reservations. If he had not, the reporters would have written about the incident and the club would have received a lot of adverse publicity.

In 1946, when Lena returned to the Copa for her second engagement, Lennie Hayton took a leave of absence from MGM to be her accompanist, and working with him convinced Lena that she would marry him. She had fought with herself over it for a long time. She had struggled to overcome her own belief, which cousin Edwina had voiced, that white men just did not marry black women. She had been suspicious of his apparent ability to understand her problems, for he was not black and couldn't possibly look at the world as she did. She tested him, and continued to test him, trying to uncover some concealed racism on his part, some cowardice about the way their relationship was viewed by the larger society. She used him, she admitted in her autobiography, as a "whipping boy," punishing him for the sins of other white men whom she had no way to hurt, denigrating him for having an easy life by the simple virtue of his color. She even accused him of being unfeeling because he didn't seem to suffer the same anguish that she did. But try as she might, she could not break him down, and once she had begun to realize it was futile to continue fighting him, she also began to realize that somehow they would eventually be together.

At that time, they were hardly seeing each other, for Lena was on the road a great deal, making up for the months when she hadn't been able to work. Lennie went back to MGM after her engagement at the Copacabana, and when Lena wasn't on the road she usually went to St. Albans, Queens, to be with Gail and with Teddy when he visited. When she did travel to the West Coast, she couldn't very well stay with him and cause the tongues of the rumormongers to start wagging again. Eventually, she purchased a house outside Los Angeles where she hoped to be able to spend time with Lennie away from prying eyes.

Lennie actually found the house, Lena's only stipulation being that it be "something away, where I won't offend anybody." He reported back that he had found amazing race hatred, and, referring to the fact that he was a Jew, said, "I'm afraid we're next." Lena said, "I've got news for you. You're now." Sections of Beverly Hills did not allow Jews in, which was ironic in an area where film studios headed by Jews were the major industry.

The house they finally bought was in Nichols Canyon in the San Fernando Valley. One of the first things they did was to have a high wall built around the property to ensure their privacy. They were there so infrequently that it was some time before the neighbors realized who owned the house. Once they learned the identify of the new owners, there was another attempt to "petition her out." This one was a little less bold, though just as deadly. Certain of Lena's neighbors formed an association of homeowners, ostensibly to do something about the gravel snatchers, men and boys who stole the pebbles and rocks with which their driveways were covered. But the main topic of discussion at meetings was the unacceptable element that was moving in. Fortunately, Lena also had some liberal neighbors who reminded the bigots that there was no restrictive covenant clause in Nichols Canyon property purchases and pointed out that judges had ruled against restrictions against Negroes in that area in two cases already—one involving singer June Richmond and one involving musician Benny Carter. One woman in particular seemed out to get her, and in an editorial the local newspaper suggested that she just forget Lena Horne. That was fine with Lena; she wanted to be forgotten. Eventually, she and Lennie were accepted. In 1951 they lost their cat, and some of the original petitioners helped to find him. And when the canyon flooded, they worked side by side with their neighbors piling sandbags.

While Lena was not appearing in movies, and while her appearances on the cabaret circuit hardly exposed her to a mass audience, she was never far from the public eye. As the top black performer in the country, she was followed diligently by the press, particularly the black press. While white reporters occasionally did stories that briefly chronicled her career, exclaimed over her beauty, and hinted at her relationship with a white man, it was the black press that chronicled her day-to-day struggles.

Life *was* a struggle for her. Appearing on Ed Gardner's radio program, she learned that listeners objected to her calling him by his first name, unless she put a "Mr." in front of it. Gardner went to the program's higher-ups on Lena's behalf, and the result was that they didn't call each other anything. There was no change on the road in the decade since Lena had first started to travel with Noble Sissle and Charlie Barnet. She and her musicians still had to contend with discrimination, even though they never ventured south of the Mason Dixon line unless specifically invited to perform for black troops. Her experiences in comparatively large, liberal cities in the Northeast would fill a book in themselves.

Finding a hotel to stay in was a constant problem. Lena's stardom helped little in gaining her entrée into establishments that were suitable for a performer of her caliber. When she and her musicians were allowed to stay in a good hotel, they were relegated to the least conspicuous and least comfortable quarters and often told to use the back door. Often, the audiences to which she played were segregated, the blacks in the balcony, the whites in the orchestra. Lena consistently informed her managers at MCA of problems she encountered on tour, suggesting that clauses be written into her contracts to forestall similar embarrassments in the future, but MCA proved to be as insensitive to her needs, though acutely sensitive to the finances of her tours, as the Louis Shurr agency had been. MCA was renowned for its service to its clients: a congratulatory telegram on opening night, and a personal representative in every city to see that the star received the proper star treatment. But Lena didn't get that kind of careful treatment; as a black, second-class citizen, she was subjected to what she felt was deliberately second-class treatment by her agents. While white clients of the agency received a congratulatory telegram on opening night, Lena received hers the second night; while the MCA representative in a particular city welcomed white stars as soon as they arrived, Lena learned to expect him to show up two or three days into her engagement.

MGM road representatives weren't much better. During World War II, airplane travel was curtailed, and even the stars who, unlike Lena, preferred to fly, found themselves taking the railroad Super Chief and having to endure a long midday stopover in Chicago. MGM employed a Chicagoan named Warren Slee for the sole purpose of entertaining stars and making arrangements for their comfort during the wait. While Slee did manage to arrange for Lena to have lunch at a good table in a prominent lakefront hotel, it wasn't the same table at which other MGM stars ate.

Only the black press chose to report regularly on the discrimination Lena suffered, and only the black press reported on the community work she continued to do when she was in Los

110

Angeles. In early April 1946 she found the time to visit the East Side Youth Center and give support to an interracial group of young people who were staging a production called *Harmony in A Flat,* and later in the month she appealed for public support for a play written by the YWCA high school club called *Going to Town.* (Frances Williams, then Frances Williams Hill, assisted in directing and otherwise preparing for the performance.) Also in April, Lena appeared with Paul Robeson and others in an appeal for funds to send food to black South Africans, whose food harvests had been devastated by a severe drought. The meeting was sponsored by the Council on African Affairs, of which Robeson was chairman, and the *Peoples Daily World,* a communist newspaper. Lena participated because of the cause, not the sponsorship, although she was a good friend of Paul Robeson and admired his principled stands. She participated in a number of benefits and meetings which Robeson supported and became known in some circles as the "female Paul Robeson."

She would have preferred to be known simply as Lena Horne, and she was involved in a variety of activities in which Robeson did not take part, among them an anti-Ku Klux Klan rally in Los Angeles in June, 1946, which had been called to protest a recent upsurge of Klan activity in the city and the apparent passivity of law enforcement officials in response. Organized by an alphabet soup of labor groups, in cooperation with Jewish groups (several of the Klan actions had been aimed at Jewish synagogues), the rally at which Lena performed was hardly an activity to be touted by MGM or MCA publicists. In fact, Lena was fairly certain that both her studio and her agency disapproved of her participation in political causes. She was also aware that there was little they could do.

Certainly they couldn't withdraw movie roles they hadn't even offered her. Word had gone down from Louis B. Mayer that she was to be allowed to accept any theater and cabaret bookings she wanted. One advantage of her limbolike status at MGM was that, while there was little that the studio would do *for* her, there was also little that it could do against her.

111

Still, Lena would have preferred fighting the studio rather than being virtually ignored; and at times it was only the presence of Lennie in Hollywood that kept her from leaving the West Coast altogether. At other times she realized that she was hardly alone in having been put in "dry dock" by MGM. Just about every other black actor had suffered the same experience—and most of the others hadn't even done anything to earn this punishment. Without making any formal announcements, the major studios had quite suddenly excised blacks from their films. This informal policy had been adopted partly in response to the protests by the NAACP and other groups that blacks were never portrayed in Hollywood films as real people, that they were only presented as stereotypical servants, jungle natives, and sporting-life types. Eager to avoid further controversy, yet unwilling to buck the standard expectations of the predominantly white movie-going audiences, the studios had simply eliminated most parts for blacks. Black parts were being routinely omitted from screenplays and, in some cases, actually cut out of books and plays that were adapted for the screen. In a couple of instances, as in the Warner Brothers productions of *Saratoga Trunk* and *Rhapsody in Blue,* roles that were originally black roles were assigned to white actors. From the middle of 1945 to autumn 1946, unemployment among black screenplayers reached unprecedented rates, and in September the predominantly white Screen Actors' Guild came out against the "silent boycott" of black actors by both major and many independent studios. After six months of pressure by black members of the guild, the board of directors had drawn up a resolution, which was presented to the membership at the September meeting by white actress Betsy Blair. The resolution called upon the Screen Actors' Guild to use all its power to oppose discrimination against blacks in the motion picture industry and called for the establishment of a special committee to meet with representatives of the Screen Writers' Guild, the Screen Directors' Guild, and the Motion Picture Producers' Association in order to "establish in the industry a policy of presenting Negro characters on the screen in the true relation they bear to American life." The resolution was passed unanimously.

Lena, who voted with gusto for the resolution, hoped that its result would indeed be more work for all the black actors, including herself. But she was twenty-nine years old now and more than a little cynical about the society into which she had been born and the field in which she worked. She was hopeful, but she didn't intend to hold her breath.

8

NOTORIOUS

IN 1947 Lena decided that her association with MGM for the previous two years had done little but restrict her career. No doubt MGM preferred a different arrangement as well, not having snapped to attention and planned projects featuring blacks in real-life roles as a result of the Screen Actors' Guild resolution, and not seeing much for Lena to do in return for her salary. Her contract came up for renewal that year, and by mutual agreement it required only ten weeks of her time each year for one picture and five more for an appearance in one theater designated by the studio. The other thirty-seven weeks she was free to do whatever she liked, including pictures for other studios, should any such offers be forthcoming.

She got her one picture for the first year of that contract out of the way in short order. In *Words and Music*, a musical biography of Richard Rodgers and Lorenz Hart, starring Mickey Rooney as Hart and Tom Drake as Rodgers, Lena played "Herself" in a singing role and didn't talk to any whites. "I'm *in* Hollywood but not *of* Hollywood because I'm Negro," she told columnists who asked her about her role in the picture. "I'd like to do a good, serious role in a mixed cast movie instead of being confined to café singer parts." Aware that her dream was not likely to be realized, she had decided to devote her time to singing.

It was rather frightening for Lena to face the prospect of twenty-five additional weeks per year when she couldn't count on any money coming in, during which she would have to support herself and her family solely by her singing. Although she had received some nice reviews over the years, she was hardly a musical superstar. She had recorded only a handful of discs: "Love Me a Little, Little, Little" in the late thirties, "Haunted Town" and "Good For Nothing Joe" with Charlie Barnet, a few sides with Teddy Wilson for Columbia while she was at Café Society, a few with Artie Shaw, a few for MGM. She'd recorded only four albums. She had never really considered herself a singer and had acquired a complex of sorts over the idea that people liked her for her looks rather than for her voice. But a few events occurred that year that bolstered her confidence.

In August the borough of Brooklyn had a Lena Horne Day. Tens of thousands of people turned out to honor her with a parade and other ceremonies, and Girls High School presented her with a certificate "In grateful recognition of the achievements of one of its distinguished daughters . . . whose talents have gladdened the hearts of multitudes." More than once Lena was moved to tears, and reporter/author Alfred Duckett, who had grown up in the Chauncey Street neighborhood, was impressed with her sincerity. "I was impressed because she remembered me, my name, because she remembered other people she had known when she was The Girl Across The Street. She recalled small incidents that one would have believed unimportant in her life."

In the fall, Lena went to Europe for the first time, and while she was unsure what her reception would be, she was optimistic that she could establish a new market for her singing and perhaps even make movies in Europe. What made the trip especially important to her was that she and Lennie had decided that, while there, they would secretly marry. There was simply no way they could get married in the United States without publicity and a storm of criticism. Their relationship was an open secret and, although they had always tried to be discreet about their private life, Lena, who had been baptized a Catholic, wore a Star of David around her neck, mentioned gefilte fish and kugel among her favorite foods, and wore a bracelet inscribed "To L. H. from L. H." But both realized that for them "living in sin" was somehow more acceptable than being legally married.

Earl Wilson devoted a substantial portion of his newspaper column of July 2, 1947, to Lena, opening it thus:

> NEW YORK.—We'll have some plain talk today with Lena Horne. Some of you'll probably ring off before you finish my piece, blazing mad.
>
> Lena's the pretty Negro actress and singer with MGM; a gal from Chauncey Street, Brooklyn, who's been fighting her way up since 16.
>
> I'd heard rumors of her romance with a talented white man. It's an open secret in Hollywood. I asked her about it.
>
> "They're open about it," people kept telling me, making me wonder whether these people meant they should be sneaky.
>
> I'm just a reportorial dictaphone, a non-partisan ringsider at life. I asked her as we sat in the Algonquin dining room, "Are you married? There've been rumors. . . ."

That long introductory disclaimer indicates, in itself, the way the nation viewed interracial relationships. In her response, Lena was more direct: "How can you defy the world about marriage when other important things such as buying a hotel room, or casting a vote, are denied you because you're a Negro?" But even as she spoke, she knew that she and Lennie were going to defy the world, in secret.

Lena and Lennie, accompanied by Tiny Kyle, her hairdresser and friend, and Luther Henderson, who was to be her accompanist, set sail for England on October 22, 1947. They had bookings in London and Paris only and so Lena chose not to bring along a large entourage but instead hired a small group of musicians in

Europe. That way, if she wasn't well received she wouldn't lose a lot of money.

No one knew how she would be received, for she was unknown in Europe. But the idea of anonymity appealed to her. She liked the idea that when the ship docked there were no newspapermen waiting for her at the pier, only a couple of young reporters from *Melody Maker,* a British jazz publication, who had heard one of her records with Charlie Barnet and a couple of her recordings with Artie Shaw. They reviewed her show at a little club in Soho, and word started to get around about the American singer who was in town. At that time, so soon after the war, very few American entertainers were in Europe, and Lena found herself an object of curiosity more because she was American than because she was black. On the whole, the English received her warmly. "The people listened to me in a *different* sort of way," she told Robert Ruark of *Esquire.* "I wasn't a curiosity, or a freak, a colored gal singing for a white audience. I was just me. Everywhere I went, they seemed to like *me* for *me.* Before that I was pretty cold on a stage. I sang mostly for myself. What happened in Europe broke down a little barrier I had rigged up for myself. My God, in London, playing a little place in Soho, they were bringing gifts to *me*—gifts when they still needed eighteen coupons for a coat. I cried a lot in London."

Actor James Mason, whom Lena and Lennie had met at the Copacabana and who had heard about their impending trip to Europe, had suggested that they look up his family and had written to his relatives to alert them to Lena's and Lennie's coming. Mason's mother had a small farm outside London, and she visited them several times, bringing eggs, which Lennie craved and which were impossible to get in London at the time. Lena was moved by this hospitality and grateful to have the opportunity to meet ordinary English folk.

There were a few unpleasant incidents. At the Piccadilly Hotel Lena had no trouble getting a room, but Tiny and Luther were denied accommodations at first. Lena protested, and eventually the hotel management acceded to her wishes. The very next night some West Indian friends were denied rooms in the same hotel, and this time Lena went public with her protest, although only the small music periodicals carried interviews with her about it. The major newspapers held her at arm's length. As she recalled in her autobiography, "The English press had been perfectly polite, but we had detected a questioning attitude, a slight air of askance, when we were seen together." When it came time to leave London for Paris, Lena was more than ready to go to a place where, she'd heard, the people couldn't care less about one's private life: "The French grant you your right to be yourself automatically. The English have to learn to respect you a little bit before they grant you that right."

They took a boat across the Channel and docked at Calais late in the afternoon, but they had to wait for a car to take them to Paris, and by the time they arrived in the City of Light it was late evening. But Lena had fallen in love with Paris long before she arrived, and just being there caused her to break into tears. They stayed at the finest hotel in Paris, no questions asked, and immediately experienced for themselves what they had heard about the French: no one paid them any particular attention.

When they arrived the city was in the midst of a series of general strikes, and the management of the Club des Champs-Elysées kept postponing Lena's opening. Lena and Lennie took advantage of the time to explore Paris—mostly on foot, because the cabdrivers were on strike. They reveled in the sheer joy of anonymity as they walked through the streets of Paris without occasioning even a second glance. There was no question, now, that they would get married in Paris.

Lena opened at the Club des Champs-Elysées in early December. A correspondent for *Time* filed this report:

> Obviously nervous, dressed in a square-shouldered white gown, Lena flashed her magnificent teeth in the spotlight and curtsied demurely. Then, as the lights went down and the rhythm began to pad out softly behind her, she slithered cosily up to the mike and began to sway. First she gave them "It Was Just One of Those

Things" in a low and sultry voice. By the time she came to the line, "Our love affair was too hot not to cool down," the French found Lena's English perfectly translatable. And when she finished "The Man I Love," and followed it with "'Deed I Do," "Stormy Weather," and "Honeysuckle Rose," she had the Parisians in her hand. They shouted, cheered, and—a rare event in France—whistled. Lena could do no wrong: she even got away with a song in schoolgirl French. After the show, admirers followed her to her dressing room. Next day *France Soir* splashed a three-column picture of her on Page One, and captioned it: "A triumph."

During Lena's two-week engagement at the club, most of the arrangements for her wedding to Lennie were completed. While in Paris, they had picked up a booking in Belgium, and the few days' engagement at a Belgian spa made their schedule a little tight. They would return to Paris the day after she finished at Chaudfontaine, near Liège, get married, and then the next morning catch the boat train to Cherbourg, where they were to board the SS *America* for home.

The group set out for Belgium, performed there for two days, then headed back to Paris. On the way, Lena brought up the subject of a wedding ring. Lennie had thought about blood tests and the ceremony, which was to be performed in one of the *arrondissements* near the hotel, but he hadn't even thought about a ring. Lena wanted one, and though they were already on a tight schedule, Lennie set out to find a ring, a task he expected would be easy. It hadn't occurred to anyone that there was a gold shortage in Paris; jewelry shop after jewelry shop sadly turned him away. Meanwhile, Lena had changed to her wedding dress (oddly enough, given that she was superstitious, it was black like her first wedding dress) and had completely packed and was wondering if she was going to be jilted. At last, however, Lennie found a jeweler with a sense of the romantic, who let him buy a plain gold band. Lennie arrived triumphantly with the ring and Lena's wedding bouquet: a bunch of violets he had bought from a street vendor. As they approached the municipal building where the ceremony was to be performed, Lena saw a young, just-married couple leaving the building with their families, and for a moment she who had worried that Lennie would be the one to back out, got cold feet. But an officious clerk rushed them in, and the mayor, a woman, made a little speech about how happy she was that they had decided to marry in her country. Lena began to cry. She cried throughout the brief ceremony, and was never quite sure afterward if it was because she was getting married to Lennie or because she was about to leave France. They had been happy in Europe, and in Paris Lena had felt free for the first time in her life.

The next morning the quartet boarded the SS *America* and set off for the United States, but Lena felt as if she were back in America long before the ship actually landed in New York. The black crew members had been denied their request to join the union, and they sent a representative to tell Lena about it. In response, Lena refused to entertain the first-class passengers at a benefit for the crew's welfare fund. There was bad feeling all around.

Lena and Lennie were in for more bad feeling when they told her family about their secret marriage. Most of her family stopped speaking to her, and her father was particularly stubborn in his refusal to understand; it was quite a while before he would have anything to do with her. Lennie's mother was supportive, Gail and Mrs. Starks were pleased to see Lena happy, and most of their friends were not privy to the secret. Frances Williams was one who was. She recalls, "I had a party here at the house [in Los Angeles]. Lena had just married Lennie then and she was radiant. She said, 'Frances, I didn't think I could marry a white man, but this man has taught me more about my people than I ever knew.'"

On their arrival back in the United States, Lena and Lennie were so busy that they had little time to think about being married or other people's reactions to it. Docking on December 22, they went immediately to St. Albans to celebrate Gail's tenth birthday and Christmas, then on December 26 they went to Manhattan. The musicians' union and the record companies were involved in a contract dispute, and the union had set a strike for January 1,

1948. The record companies, facing an indeterminate period when they would be able to produce no recordings, wanted to get as much material recorded as possible, and Lena and Lennie spent four days straight recording their complete repertory. After that, Lennie had to return to Los Angeles and MGM, and Lena had to go out on the road.

Years after Lennie Hayton's death, Lena admitted that she hadn't loved him when she married him. She had married him because she needed him. She needed someone to lean on, someone who would take care of her. She wasn't thinking of depending on him financially: Lennie wasn't particularly interested in money, wouldn't work for people he didn't like, and refused to grind out songs. Lena didn't expect him to support her, even after they were married, for the children whose expenses had to be paid were hers by another man and it was a matter of principle for her to take care of them herself ("I was always such a 'gentleman' about such things," she says). Lena needed Lennie's emotional support and musical sustenance; it was his unquestioning giving of the things she needed that caused her to love him. While she may not have loved him at the beginning, being married to Lennie gave Lena the sense of security she needed to pursue a career as a cabaret singer. With Lennie behind her, she began to feel that she could make it as a singer. After all, he hated singers, but he had taught her anyway. And he had devised a repertoire of songs that were appropriate for her voice, not just currently popular songs but obscure show songs and noncommercial classics, which she sang in a way that was reminiscent of saloon singing. He had told her at the beginning that she was strong on drama and weak on vocals, and they spent years building up her voice. He had taught her how to listen to music, to understand the structure, what the composer or musician was trying to do. She embarked on her new singing career with considerably more knowledge about music and with a modicum of confidence about audiences' interest in her voice as well as in looks.

Over the next months she performed in countless clubs in cities across the Northeast, northern Midwest, and on the West Coast.

By October 1948 *Life* magazine was calling her the season's top nightclub star: "For months Manhattan's nightclub owners had held their heads in agony and kept their bankruptcy plans in readiness. Business was horrible. Then Lena Horne, the singer whose beautiful face and wriggly figure have made her the season's top nightclub attraction, moved into the Copacabana. Business boomed to an all-time record: $60,000 a week. The Copa's managers began humming Lena's hit tune, 'Do I love you. . . ? Honey! 'Deed I do.'" Performing in New York was a delight to Lena, for she felt very much at home. Gail was there, and Teddy when he visited, and if the people of the city were not exactly French in their attitude toward blacks, they were quite liberal compared to people elsewhere in the United States.

Performing in other cities was fraught with the same old problems Lena had experienced as a black entertainer on the road, and no matter how many management changes she made she could not forestall the painful and degrading encounters to which she could not, and would not, ever become accustomed. Tired of MCA's lack of concern for her, Lena bought out her contract with that agency. On Lennie's advice, instead of hiring another large agency, she chose, instead, to hire a personal road manager and to give the business of booking her to smaller agencies.

Ralph Harris became her road manager. A friend of Lennie's, he had worked as a performer and a song-plugger for record companies, among numerous other jobs. He worked for Lena in return for nothing but expenses while she paid off her debt to MCA, and during that time he helped her more than all of her previous agents had, despite their hefty fees.

Lena had been vigilant about playing to integrated audiences wherever possible; but she had learned that some club and hotel owners would assure her that there would be no discrimination and then use the tactic of having "no record" of the blacks who showed up to claim their reservations. Ralph Harris hit upon the idea of having black friends call for reservations; he'd then show up with a list and stand next to the maître d' with that list, so there would be no "confusion" about who had reservations. He also used his show-business experience to outwit a few racist hotel managers who thought they could have Lena perform while denying service to her musicians. In 1948 Lena was the first black to perform at a large hotel in St. Louis. She was also allowed to enter the restaurants in the hotel; but her musicians were not granted the same courtesy, and so Lena didn't take advantage of the privilege. Ralph Harris wasn't one to accept this sort of situation meekly. He took it upon himself to march into the bar, order a trayful of drinks, then march through the lobby, into the front elevator, and up to the room where Lena was staying. He did it all so conspicuously that other guests began to wonder why a white man, who must be a paying guest, couldn't get a waiter to serve him. The management was clearly embarrassed. Lena went over extremely well at the hotel, and the management was so pleased that it rescinded its rule against serving the musicians in the dining rooms; but Lena's group had so enjoyed Harris's performance and the embarrassment it caused that they preferred to be served as before.

But segregation and racists were not always so easy to outwit, and Lena found herself bucking the system straight-on, without cleverness or guile, more often than not. She filed suits against a restaurant in Chicago that barred her entry in September 1949 and against theaters that would not admit blacks to see her performances. She always took such actions as an individual, not as some spokeswoman for her race, and when asked to behave as a symbol she generally refused, leading to accusations by black organizations and the black press that she was being insulated by people like Lennie and Ralph Harris.

Lena hardly felt insulated. Cabaret singing was, in her opinion, the most exposed type of entertaining possible. "I don't know how to say it—it's so physical, it's all body," she tried to explain to Seymour Peck of *The New York Times* back in the 1950s. "There's whiskey, there's sex, there's something that is experienced only when people are drinking in a night club and having a good time. There are so many ways they look at you, their emotions aren't disciplined . . . it's you and you are at the mercy of their thoughts."

The schedule itself was killing: three shows a night, seven nights a week, often not getting to bed until 6 A.M., having only about two hours to call her own each day; traveling on trains and buses from one city to another, having to worry about eating right and getting enough sleep, somehow, so that her voice wouldn't suffer; on the road for weeks at a time, and when she got a break, being in conflict about whether to spend the time in New York with her family or with Lennie on the West Coast. Lena paid dearly for her success as a cabaret singer, and so did the people who loved her.

After a couple of years on the road, Lena yearned for a way to make money while staying in one spot. Realizing that the only way she could do this was to appear in a movie, she went to MGM determined to land a movie role and hoping that, by her sheer presence around the studio and in Hollywood, she could influence the studio bosses to consider her more seriously. Perhaps the old adage, "out of sight, out of mind," had been operating; perhaps visibility would enhance her chances for a film part.

But Lena found Hollywood filmdom even more hostile to blacks than before. With the help of the makeup created especially for her by Max Factor—Light Egyptian—MGM didn't need beautiful, light-complected "colored girls" to play the parts of mulattoes, it could use whites. For a remake of *White Cargo*, MGM chose Hedy Lamarr, in Light-Egyptian-face, to play the half-caste Tondelayo. Over at Twentieth Century-Fox there was a new film in the works about a light-skinned woman who passes for white. It was called *Pinky* and Ethel Waters was already set to star. Lena, whose contract with MGM allowed her to seek roles in movies produced by other studios, would have been perfect for the title role; and she would even have considered working with Ethel Waters again if she could only have had the luxury of being settled in one place for a time. But the role of Pinky went to a white actress, Jeanne Crain.

Back at MGM a movie version of *Show Boat* was in the planning stages. Lena had been denied the opportunity to play the mulatto, Julie, in the Broadway revival a few years earlier, but she hoped that the unpleasantness of that period could be treated as water under the bridge. Lena believed then, and continued to believe for a long time afterward, that she had been born to play Julie. But once again she was denied that opportunity. The role was given to Ava Gardner, made-up with Light Egyptian.

What softened this blow for Lena somewhat was that she genuinely liked Ava Gardner, a young MGM starlet from the South with whom she had become friendly the moment they met. Like Tallulah Bankhead, daughter of a Southern Congressman, who in Lena's early years in Hollywood came right out and told Lena that her features were too Caucasian and that she preferred *her* Negroes to look like the happy, dark girls back home, Ava Gardner had a down-home honesty that Lena could appreciate.

Frances Williams felt the same way about Ava as Lena did. Williams had a role in *Show Boat* and got to know Gardner in the course of filming the movie. "Ava Gardner didn't begin to have the equipment as an actress that Lena had. A black woman should do that part," says Williams. "But Ava was very honest, and she had no illusions about her acting abilities. She would say, 'Frances, I don't know a damn thing about what I'm doing. You know I left the country when I was thirteen—they said I'd make a good actress. They put me up there and told me to hold my head on the side and open my eyes slowly, and that's all I'd have to do.' All through [the filming of] *Show Boat* she said things like that."

To Lena, Ava complained that the studio made her listen to Lena's records and kept telling her to "play it like Lena would." Lena simply could not resent a girl who was so honest, and when Ava got into trouble with the studio for her "independent and free" life-style, Lena could only applaud her for her gumption. They spent many a night in the house in Nichols Canyon, barefoot, sitting on the floor, drinking and laughing about the pretenses of Hollywood, and listening to jazz. Ava was a real jazz buff; among her several husbands was Artie Shaw.

The one part Lena managed to get was in a thoroughly forgettable film titled *The Duchess of Idaho*. Released in 1950, it starred Esther Williams, Van Johnson, John Lund, and Paula Raymond, and "featured" Lena Horne in yet another easily cut singing bit. Clearly, there was little hope for Lena to renew her movie career, despite her success as a cabaret singer. She didn't know how much of the cold-shouldering by the studios was due to her relationship with Lennie and how much of it was due to the racial climate in the country. She no longer cared. Her experiences back in Hollywood led her to conclude, at last, that she was not to have a career in films; the reason hardly mattered. What did matter was that she stop hoping, put that particular dream to rest, and stop wasting time. Her energy would be far better concentrated on her singing. However, she developed a coldness and a bitterness inside that prevented her from giving to her audiences the little that she had to give. She was tired—tired of the road, tired of keeping secret her marriage to Lennie. She needed a change, so Lennie, who had continued to work for MGM and whose work in *On the Town* had won him an Oscar in 1949, arranged for another leave of absence from MGM, this time for six months, and they planned a second, longer European tour.

Once the plans to go to Europe had been made, Lena revealed the fact that she and Lennie had been married secretly in 1947. The first news photograph of them together appeared in late June 1950. She made no startling public announcement, just began to tell interviewers, when the subject arose. Even so, the public reaction was vituperative. Some of the letters Lena received were so hate-filled that Lennie and Ralph Harris wouldn't let her see them, and Ralph contacted the postal service about two or three of the letter writers, who were warned that legal action would be taken against them if they did not cease their hate campaign. By that time Lena and Lennie had fled to Europe.

This time, Lena didn't have the luxury of anonymity in Europe, but this time she needed the adoration of Europeans to offset the degradation she had suffered in her own country. In London the Palladium had her name engraved on a bronze plate for her dressing room; after she attracted record-breaking crowds, that theater presented her with an expensive car in appreciation. From there she toured the provinces for the first time, where she encountered, also for the first time ever, huge crowds waiting for her and following her wherever she went. In Glasgow, the police were called in to maintain order. Paris greeted her as an old friend. One luxurious nightclub where she appeared had her image etched on the champagne glasses. In Scandinavia, where she and Lennie spent most of their six-month tour, they found crowds, too, but much more polite ones. In Stockholm, two thousand people applauded her when she stepped into a cab. Inside the theaters in Sweden, the audience was hushed, respectful. Instead of cheering her, they threw violets, and at the end of her show the stage was literally covered with them. In Scandinavia and Belgium, she found that the audiences knew all of her songs and showed the most intelligent appreciation of jazz. Scandinavians were also the most open about their appreciation of Lena's beauty. In Sweden, a beautiful blonde told her, "After the boys here went crazy for you in *Cabin in the Sky*, all the girls rushed out to buy the darkest makeup they could find."

Europe was just what Lena needed after her two years on the road in the United States and her brush-off from Hollywood. As she told Robert Ruark of *Esquire*, "Everywhere I went it was beautiful. I was eating beautiful food, and drinking beautiful wine. Everything smelled beautiful to me. I dug it the most. I *fit*. And then I began to think that in a lot of ways the attitude I liked best was just what I liked best about home. It's funny, but the Europe thing made me happier at home. Seems like I had to get off from it to see it. This country, I mean. The Problem didn't seem so big any more. You might say that Europe straightened me out."

Fresh from, and refreshed by, the long sojourn in Europe, Lena returned to her life as a cabaret singer on the road, or, as she put it, "in the rooms." By now she was a big enough star so that she didn't have to accept bookings in places where she or her musicians would encounter any undue unpleasantness, and she did not accept them. By late 1950, in fact, Lena had hit the big time—which was the claim Las Vegas made for itself even before it was really true. In December she opened at The Sands hotel, which *Life* magazine covered with a several-page color spread. At the time Las Vegas was only beginning to be a major attraction, but it paid big money and it had glitter galore. That year she was also the subject of a biography by Helen Greenberg and Carlton Moss titled *In Person: Lena Horne.*

Lena played only the top night spots, unless she chose to play elsewhere. She played the Clover Club in Miami, the Copa in New York, the poshest clubs in all the major liberal cities. In 1951, she worked twenty weeks and grossed $175,000; in 1952 she had upped her fee to $12,500 weekly. If that kind of fee put her in clubs that most black people couldn't afford, she couldn't help it. She didn't try to be white—refusing many invitations to white homes and keeping mainly to herself—but she didn't put herself on the line because she was black. She did not deliberately court trouble because of her color or get involved in racial problems in a city just because she happened to be there. In Miami in 1952 there had been an increase in Klan activity and even bombings in black neighborhoods, but Lena didn't make any public statements.

That is not to say that she gave up her long-time association with the NAACP or other organizations. She often performed free at benefits. In 1952, she and Lennie went on a trip to Europe and Israel, and in Israel, which was celebrating its fourth birthday as a nation, she did one free benefit for every commercial concert she gave. Returning from Israel, she went to her engagement in Miami and while there performed at a kickoff benefit for the Bonds for Israel drive. She hadn't lost her public spirit, she had just gotten tired of the "Negro problem," or any other problem, for that matter.

She told Robert Ruark, "Man, I am fed up with problems. What I want to be is happy as I can on the best terms I can. That's happy enough. I have never been able to understand where skin color was much more important than hair color, but I guess it is, and it's strange that my daughter will probably live to see a world where they pay off on what you are instead of what you have to wear to match your skin. I am just looking for some peace."

9

RED SCARE

IF Lena Horne was tired of problems and eager for some simple peace in 1952, she had good reason. Over the previous decade she had been forced to fight discrimination on the road, to endure acrimony from those for whom interracial marriages were anathema, and, just recently, to suffer the ignominy of being blacklisted as a communist sympathizer, although she had never been publicly accused of leftist leanings nor called upon to answer any formal charges. As such, she suffered no more than hundreds of other entertainers; but being blacklisted on top of everything else made understandable her desire to simply shut out all the problems.

The Red Scare had hit Hollywood shortly after the war, in the same year as Lena and Lennie were married in Paris. Acting on the premise that subversives within the motion picture industry were flooding the country with films that were rife with communist propaganda, the House Un-American Activities Committee (HUAC) had opened public hearings in Washington, DC, in October. The first witnesses were people in Hollywood who confirmed the committee's suspicions, among them Lela Rogers, mother of Ginger Rogers, who testified that the original script for the film *Tender Comrade* had called for her daughter to speak the line: "Share and share alike—that's democracy," and that her daughter had refused to do so. Other witnesses who were considered "friendly" by the committee included actors Adolphe Menjou, Robert Taylor, Gary Cooper, and Ronald Reagan, also an actor and then president of the Screen Actors' Guild. Although few other than these witnesses actually named names, they supported the committee's impression of communist influence in Hollywood by saying that there was a small group of people who did seem bent on exerting their influence in ways that seemed "associated" with the Communist Party. Then the committee called a group of "unfriendly" witnesses—people whose communist leanings seemed fairly evident to the committee and to its sources, who seemed to have laid the major blame on writers. The group included one director, Edward Dmytryk, one producer, Adrian Scott, and eight writers: John Howard Lawson, Dalton Trumbo, Ring Lardner, Jr., Albert Maltz, Alvah Bessie, Herbert Biberman, Lester Cole, and Samuel Ornitz. Most of them refused to testify, claiming that the First Amendment guaranteed their right not to incriminate themselves. All ten were cited for contempt of Congress, convicted in trials in U.S. District Court, and given jail sentences and fines. All appealed their convictions, and the case went all the way to the Supreme Court. The Court declined to review the case, and in June 1950 the group who had become known as the Hollywood Ten surrendered and began serving their sentences.

Charges of communist activity and subversive filmmaking in Hollywood were naturally bad for business, and soon after members of the Hollywood Ten began to appear before the committee, some fifty prominent movie producers met secretly at the Waldorf-Astoria in New York and agreed that the only way to deal with the accusations of communist influence in Hollywood was to police the industry more strictly than HUAC could. Accordingly, they announced that all ten of the accused witnesses were fired and would not be rehired until they had cleared themselves of contempt of Congress, had been found not guilty, or had declared under oath that they were not communists. Further, all other suspected communists in the industry would be considered ineligible for employment until they repented and renounced their communist affiliations.

By 1950, the Hollywood blacklist had snowballed to include hundreds of people, and by 1951 the various unions in the industry had bowed to the pressure of the Red Scare, which roared across Hollywood like wildfire. Friendships with communists, association with left-leaning organizations, lending one's name to causes supported by communists—all such activities rendered one suspect. Lena Horne was a friend of Paul Robeson and she'd been called his female counterpart. She had been a member of the NAACP since the age of two (her grandmother had enrolled her) and a member of the Hollywood Independent Citizens Committee of the Arts, Sciences, and Professions since arriving on the Coast in the early 1940s. As she puts it, Lena also "belonged to all the same outfits that Mrs. Roosevelt did." Now she found herself drummed out of the Screen Actors' Guild. "This shook up the bosses at MGM and they insisted I write the union a letter clearing myself," she told Arthur Bell of the *Village Voice* in 1981. "The letter said, 'I'm black. I have these friends. I don't know anything about their politics.' Nevertheless, MGM didn't put me back to work."

Events seemed to conspire to force Lena to leave Hollywood. In 1952 a flood washed a chunk of mountain down onto the Nichols Canyon house. In 1953 Lennie's contract as premier arranger with the Arthur Freed unit at MGM ran out, and the cold shoulder he had received at the studio as a result of his marriage to Lena left him disinclined to seek its renewal. By this time he preferred to work on the road with Lena anyway. They decided to relocate to New York.

Back in New York they ran into another set of problems. Mrs. Starks informed them that it was time for her to resume her own life with her family, and Lena could hardly argue against that; she had been available when Lena needed her most. Lena hired another housekeeper for a time; but as she settled into the household in St. Albans, Queens, and had an opportunity to observe her daughter and her daughter's day-to-day life, she found she didn't like Gail's environment. Gail had gotten into a clique that reminded Lena of her own childhood friends in Brooklyn, and she didn't want Gail to be in a setting that she considered limited and snobbish.

Since she and Lennie hardly wanted to live in the kind of neighborhood that she remembered in Brooklyn, Lena got rid of the house in St. Albans without making suitable arrangements elsewhere. She expected to be able to find an apartment in Manhattan, but she soon learned that Jim Crow was still roosting in Manhattan luxury apartment buildings. She and Lennie had three strikes against them: she was black, he was Jewish, and they were married to each other. Every door they tried was closed to them, and Lena was particularly peeved when they were refused an apartment in the Eldorado on Central Park West that was owned by C. M. "Daddy" Grace, the black religious leader who had made millions from black people.

For Lena and Lennie the inability to find an apartment in Manhattan was frustrating, but it wasn't crucial—they were planning to be on the road a lot, and in Europe as often as possible. They could operate out of a suite in the Park Sheraton Hotel at 55th and Broadway, a haven for show people. But they couldn't leave Gail in a hotel. Thus, Gail lived for a time with a friend and attended a progressive school, and when the little girl was unhappy at school Lena arranged for her to attend a boarding school in Poughkeepsie, New York, putting aside the guilt she felt at not being a proper mother to the child over whom she had year-round custody.

Finding a place to live in New York was only one of the problems Lena encountered. She also found that she was blacklisted from appearing on radio and the infant medium of television, both of which were centered in New York at that time. The radio and TV blacklist was even harder to combat than the Hollywood blacklist because it was not centered in established organizations like the Screen Actors' Guild. The blacklists for these industries were drawn up by private, self-appointed agencies that compiled lists of personae non grata and provided information from their voluminous files on these persons not only to the networks but also to companies that regularly advertised on radio and television. They charged a fee for this service to both the networks and the advertisers—entrepreneurship is always alive and well in America. Once in New York, Lena found that she was listed in *Red Channels,* a publication that had been devised by those agencies, and because her name was in it she couldn't get any broadcast work to speak of. Tex McCrary and Jinx Falkenburg had a local daytime television show in New York at the time, and they were the only broadcasters who invited her to appear.

Lena's dream had been to settle in New York with Lennie, to get a nice, big apartment where Gail and a housekeeper/babysitter could feel at home while she and Lennie were on the road. Lena wanted a place where she could entertain friends and family. (Her father had finally accepted the marriage, although it took him three years.) She hoped to get enough work on radio and TV and even perhaps on Broadway to enable them to settle down a bit and live a semblance of a normal life. When she found that this comparatively unambitious dream was impossible for her, she lost her spirit for a time. As she later described it, she turned cold and distant.

She was talking primarily about her performing persona and about her relationship with her audiences. She worked just as hard, if not harder, rehearsing for her appearances. In fact, she became a stickler for professionalism and insisted on more, and longer, rehearsals. She was determined that there would be one area of her life where she could not be faulted in any way—and if she were, then it would be entirely her own responsibility. Only up on a stage, singing, was she relatively free of arbitrary pronouncements about her politics or her color. And she used that stage both to throw at her predominantly white audiences all the sex and earthiness that, being black, she was accused of anyway,

135

and to withhold even a modicum of sharing with them unless they allowed themselves to see her as a human being. Ralph Harris tried to explain it to Robert Ruark: "Lena works on a crowd's insides, until the crowd is giving her as much as she gives the crowd. The crowd knows it. She is not singing at them, and they realize they've got to give something back or it's no dice. She's crystallizing something for them that needs *their* help. They don't get whatever-it-is until they throw something back for Horne." During the early 1950s, Lena was successful enough in getting back something from most of her audiences that she continued giving, a little. But if she'd had the means she wouldn't have played Las Vegas, for there, in her opinion, the crowd gave back nothing. They had one thing on their minds: gambling, which prevented them from responding to anything else. Lena played The Sands hotel in Las Vegas consistently during the years that she was blacklisted from performing in film or on radio and TV, and she contends that if one had to play Las Vegas, The Sands was one of the better places. Still, in her opinion Las Vegas was the pits for a serious singer; she would have turned down invitations to go there if it hadn't been one of the few places where the Red Scare tide seemed unable to encroach. The color to which the Las Vegas bosses felt a total allegiance was unalterably green.

Denied work in radio, TV, films, and recording, Lena spent even more time on the road in the early and mid-1950s than she had before, but after Lennie left MGM in 1953 she at least had his company, and that made road life easier. Her road routine—sleep late, lunch, read, talk, study, shop, Martini, dress, show, rest, show, brandy, book, bed—was not so much disturbed as enhanced by his presence. She had someone with whom to share the routine. Lennie added his own activities to the schedule, among them the playing of Scrabble. Frances Williams recalls, "Many times as I traveled around the country, I would land in the same place as they were and we would meet. We'd eat and play Scrabble together—Lennie was a very good Scrabble player, and we could play until five the next morning."

While not happy to be confined to the "rooms," Lena, forced to make her living as a cabaret singer, determined to be the best she could be. She was a consummate professional who preferred at least an hour of practice per day and sometimes much more. She asked more work of her musicians than was normally required of sidemen, but she paid them more than traveling musicians usually received (her payroll for piano, drums, and bass fiddle ran to $1000 per week). She worked tirelessly on phrasing, trimming what she called "slop" out of a phrase that to the uninitiated sounded perfect already. She worked on a song until it became so distinctively hers that anyone else's rendition—and plenty of singers recorded songs that she first revived—seemed vacuous by comparison. Certainly less sexy. Sexiness in her singing was Lena's trademark, but the subtle aloofness and detachment she maintained rendered them insouciant, risqué, but not indecent. Wrote Robert Ruark in *Esquire*:

> She does not flatly sing suggestive stuff, and makes no obvious pass at male audiences. She does rather direct her mood at women, who seem more allied with her in a general insinuation that true love is harder on girls than it is on boys. . . . What Miss Horne offers . . . is sex . . . in such a various shading of sexiness that you can't nail it on any terms except the listener's terms. . . . The mood is there for you to identify, and most of the time it seems to be *your* mood.

Throughout the 1950s, even though she was a major star, Lena continued to encounter racial discrimination. In February 1955, for example, the Royal York Hotel in Miami Beach canceled her and Lennie's accommodations without explanation. Although the club at which she was scheduled to sing, the Copa City, had no connection with the hotel, Lena canceled the club engagement. "They'll grow up," she remarked, shrugging her shoulders. She didn't intend to expend needless energy fighting, or worrying about being unfair to the club because of the actions of the hotel. Besides, she may have hoped that the city, wishing to avoid such unpleasant publicity in the future, would bring pressure to bear on the hotel and others who persisted in their restrictive policies. They could do the fighting for her.

The discrimination Lena had suffered because of her left-wing associations, however, began to lift by the mid-1950s. In 1955 MGM called her back to Hollywood to appear in *Meet Me in Las Vegas*, released in 1956, which starred Cyd Charisse and Dan Dailey. Having played Las Vegas frequently since 1950, Lena was a natural to do a musical segment in the film. Lennie arranged and conducted her number, and the two hoped to get more film work, for it would enable them to settle in one place for a while. They'd been living out of suitcases and hotel rooms since giving up the houses in California and New York. But no other offers for film work were forthcoming.

About a year later, Lena finally managed to get her name removed from the *Red Channels* blacklist. Lennie's agent told her about the involved and rather circuitous process by which her name could be cleared: She would have to meet with the head of one of the large theatrical unions, who in turn would arrange for her to appear before one of the informal clearance groups, which had the power to see that her name was removed from the list. Ridiculous as the process seemed, by that time Lena was willing to go through it. Accordingly, she met with the union boss, who directed her to a different second step than she had been led to expect: she had to meet George Sokolsky, a political columnist, who apparently was eager to help her. He assured her that he understood what she had gone through because he had once been married to a Chinese woman. Lena was never certain what that had to do with her case but was willing to accept the existence of a tenuous connection if it would help her. To her considerable relief, she didn't have to go before any clearance group. Sokolsky and, she suspects, Tex McCrary and Ed Sullivan, who wanted her as a guest on his television program, managed to persuade the man who ran *Red Channels* to drop her name from the list. Shortly afterward she began to receive a few invitations to appear on television—from Sullivan; from Steve Allen, host of the

"Tonight Show"; and from variety show hosts, among them Perry Como.

Also around 1956 she and Lennie got their long-sought Manhattan apartment, although they had to go to Europe to get it. That year they went on their third European tour, this time taking along Gail and Teddy, who at eighteen and sixteen were old enough to appreciate and benefit from the trip. Because she was with her entire family, and because her children behaved in a manner that made her proud, Lena especially enjoyed this tour. Finding a New York apartment because of the trip made it exceptional in her memory. The conductor, José Iturbi, provided the apartment. He was in Paris when they were, and he approached Ralph Harris with the idea of Lena's doing a benefit concert for his Rochester (New York) Symphony Orchestra. Initially, Harris turned him down, for Lena's tight schedule didn't allow for unlimited benefit performances, and she was already committed to perform free of charge for causes that she held dear. Iturbi was persistent, however, and in the course of their discussion Harris learned that the conductor was trying to get out of the lease he held on a Manhattan apartment where he rarely stayed and which was too expensive for him to keep empty. As a result, Lena agreed to do the benefit, and Iturbi let them take over his lease.

The apartment was in a large prewar building at 300 West End Avenue. The ceilings were high, the rooms large; the place was big enough for Gail when she was on vacation from Radcliffe, for Teddy when he visited, for her father when he came, for their huge collection of 78 rpm records, and for Lena to invite uncles and friends and cook them a big meal at holiday time. At last they had their home.

Lena enjoyed the apartment so much that she longed to be able to stay in New York for a time, but there wasn't enough work for her in the city to enable her to remain there steadily. She did sign a recording contract with RCA Victor in 1956, and recorded for the first time in five years. *Stormy Weather* and *Lena Horne at the Coconut Grove* did very well. "I never particularly liked the way I sounded on records," she told an interviewer in February 1957.

"But now, with hi-fi and all, I think I sound better. Records are hard—I'm a visual performer, and records aren't visual. I have to try and get personal on an impersonal record. . . . It's important to a singer—even a nightclub singer—to have hits. It makes it easier on the floor. When they hear a song they've heard on the radio, they know it and it gives you a head start."

Unfortunately, Lena's records were not sufficiently big hits to allow her to stay in New York. Nor was television a realistic possibility for her in the mid-1950s. The black presence on television was minimal and confined almost exclusively to variety and talk shows, on which any one performer could appear only so often. Only Eddie Anderson, as Rochester on the "Jack Benny Show," had managed to get work in a series. In 1957, NBC tried an experiment by giving Nat "King" Cole a fifteen-minute show, and Lena hoped that if this show were successful she might be given the same opportunity. Unfortunately, no sponsor would go near Cole's show, fearing reprisals from Southern consumers. In the club business, although New York boasted more clubs than any other city in the country, Lena couldn't play any one of them, or even the city, too frequently for fear of being overexposed. A show on Broadway was the only possibility she had.

In the early 1950s, groups like Actors' Equity, Chorus Equity, the Dramatists' Guild, and the League of New York Theatres had been spurred by their black members to draw up a statement similar to that which had been passed by the Screen Actors' Guild —a statement that called for blacks to be portrayed in roles that reflected their participation in American life—but the statement had little effect. Broadway seemed a cold White Way for blacks in the mid-1950s. Nevertheless, Lena received many scripts for plays and she read them with great interest, hoping to find a vehicle that would be suitable for her. But she rejected them all. In some instances, she didn't like the character she was asked to play or felt that the story fostered the old, unfortunate stereotypes. In other instances, she was unmoved by the score—primarily the lyrics, since she didn't read music. She even declined invitations to appear in shows whose books and music she liked, for fear that they were insufficiently commercial and wouldn't succeed on Broadway. While aware that any show was a risky venture, Lena felt that she would have to put a great deal at risk herself if she agreed to do one. She would have to cancel engagements, let her musicians go, and spend weeks rehearsing for scale wages. Then, if the show flopped, she'd have nothing in return for her time and trouble except new problems hiring other musicians and getting a new club act ready. She believed she could only justify accepting a Broadway role if she liked the book and the music and was fairly certain of its commercial promise.

In the spring of 1957 Lena opened at the Empire Room of the Waldorf-Astoria, where for eight weeks she drew a record audience for her two nightly shows. The album she recorded for RCA Victor, *Lena Horne at the Waldorf-Astoria,* later became the largest-selling record by a female artist in the history of RCA. During her engagement, Harold Arlen came to hear her and to offer her a role in a show for which he and lyricist Yip Harburg had written the score. It was to be called *Jamaica.* Immediately, Lena felt that two of her requirements for an acceptable Broadway show had already been met: if Harold Arlen had written the music, she wanted to sing it, and given the then current calypso craze, the show had excellent commercial potential. When she read the script written by Harburg and Fred Saidy, however, she was disappointed. It was a rather weak story about a simple Caribbean fisherman and his restless girl friend who dreams of the bright lights of New York, and Lena immediately expressed her disapproval of the character, Savanna, whom she had been asked to play. Arlen and Harburg explained that the show had been written originally for Harry Belafonte, the top male entertainer in the calypso style, but that he had too many commitments to undertake the role of the fisherman. They had then approached Lena, feeling that to be successful the show needed a major star. Naturally, they would change the script and strengthen the character of Savanna. With that assurance, Lena decided to take whatever risks were necessary and commit herself at last to a Broadway show.

141

In June 1957 Lena and Lennie were in Hollywood, playing the Coconut Grove. While there, Lena celebrated her fortieth birthday and announced that she was retiring from the nightclub circuit for a while. "The reason I'm giving up clubs as well as a full-time career is that I don't want to be an older woman singer," she explained to UPI correspondent Aline Mosby. "I don't think there's anything attractive about an older woman singing about sex and romance. I'll feel more graceful when I'm older if I'm working in the theater instead of singing about how crazy some man makes me feel. . . . I'm a little tired of clubs and I feel good about leaving them. I was in a rut. I began to know all the headwaiters and their children!"

Lena had been preparing for middle age since she was about twenty-eight. Lennie had teased her about it, but she had been quite serious. To her mind, when one reached middle age, one said good-bye to sexiness. No doubt, having been on the road for close to a decade, she was feeling every one of her forty years. She had a daughter in college, a son about to enter college—in no time at all, she probably would be a grandmother. She didn't want to be a grandmother singing sexy songs in some nightclub. She expected to continue to play clubs occasionally—"as long as I still have teeth"—but she was firmly convinced that an "old broad" trying to be sexy would not be able to make a living in the rooms. She had to get into something else.

By the late summer of 1957 the casting of *Jamaica* had been completed. Ricardo Montalban would play the fisherman, Ossie Davis and Josephine Premice were in the supporting cast. Lena, who hadn't appeared on Broadway since the short-lived *Blackbirds of 1939*, now faced what she considered to be one of the biggest challenges of her professional life. She felt simultaneously exhilarated and depressed.

Her exhilaration derived from the experience of being "part" of something, which she had not felt in the cabarets and certainly not in the majority of the movies she had done. In the cabarets she had been completely alone, part of her own musical ensemble, to be sure, but very exposed and alone in front of the audience, at the mercy of their thoughts. In all her movies, except for the two with all-black casts, it had been understood by all that her scenes were not integral to the plot. As she explained to Seymour Peck of *The New York Times*, "No one bothered to put me in a movie where I talked to anybody, where some thread of the story might be broken if I were cut. I had no communication with anybody. I began to feel depressed about it, wasted emotionally. . . . Here, doing a show, I'm part of some other people, part of a story, part of a problem being worked out by all. It's very comforting."

She was depressed because she felt that she had never really learned how to act and questioned her ability, at forty, to learn. She hired an acting coach, John Lehne. The director, Robert Lewis, was helpful. The cast, young and old, well known and unknown, were supportive. Still, Lena couldn't bring herself to relax and give herself to the role. The fact that the role was never rewritten to suit her contributed to her inability to make it her own, and she couldn't seem to take the necessary command to alter the role so that it did fit. Being a passionate rehearser didn't seem to help in this situation as it had in her cabaret work. Rehearsing her nightclub act, she'd had a natural feeling for the material, and it mattered little that she couldn't read a note of music. She couldn't summon the same natural wisdom about how best to deliver a line in the play, what nuance of voice best invited a laugh. At the end of a day's rehearsals she would return home so frustrated and frightened that she would burst into tears as soon as she closed the apartment door. Sighed Robert Lewis, "Lena's a self-castigator."

When the show went to Philadelphia for trials in early October, Lena was feeling singularly unconfident, and the reviews weren't good. Lena Horne, who from a nightclub stage could manipulate an audience like very few of her peers, went stone-cold in front of an audience on the other side of the footlights. Her performance was wooden, and since, as the star, she controlled the mood of the rest of the cast, the play came off as lacking in warmth and spontaneity.

The ensemble went on to Boston, where correspondent Peck

143

arrived on the scene to do interviews. Robert Lewis expressed a sort of fatherly exasperation with Lena: "Why one who combines every quality should question herself so, I'll never know," he said. "She's glamorous, as you see. She's beautiful all day long and shines twenty-four hours. Talent? She's electrifying. And she's modest; you have to build her confidence. She wants to kill herself when she makes a mistake. She's never given a bit of the trouble a star can give. On opening night in Philadelphia her clothes weren't ready. She pinned herself into stuff, improvised. Never a beef, not a word. Another star wouldn't have gone on . . . Lena didn't even know she was allowed to complain."

Peck was waiting for Lena in her dressing room when she returned from her performance one night, and as if scripted to conform with Lewis's appraisal, she announced, "I hate myself! . . . hearing myself act. In cabarets I never spoke in my act; what could I say that wasn't said better in the songs I sang? Now I listen to myself speak onstage and I think, 'Oh, God.' I know when I'm ruining a couple of laughs. Is my Jamaican accent right or does it sound Southern?"

In the report he filed, Peck wrote that he had detected an exultant note in Lena's lamentation, and he was right on target. In Boston she got better. She found a way to deliver a line that had more effect, she got a laugh where she had not gotten one before. Audiences were warmer. Crowds waited outside the theater not only to see the famous Lena Horne but to congratulate her on her performance. Peck noted that on the night he observed her she thanked the crowd for waiting.

Critics were not as kind as the crowds, but Lena had learned years earlier not to read reviews of her work but to judge her reception by her audiences' behavior. Her director and the rest of the cast chose not to assault her fragile confidence by giving her any inkling that the reviews had been, at best, lukewarm.

On arrival in New York, however, Lena mounted her own aggressive assault on her confidence. Boston and Broadway were, in her mind, two different animals, and despite the phenomenal advance ticket sales amounting to $1,200,000, due largely to her presence in the cast, she had again descended into a mood of self-castigation so severe that even Robert Lewis, who by this time considered himself fairly adept at "uncastigating" her nightly, was worried. In the two benefit performances given before the actual opening night, Lena froze, and she had enough years of experience reading an audience to know that they were disappointed. Thus, when on November 30, 1957, the actual opening night came, Lena was so afraid of bombing that she could no longer handle the fear. Something inside her brain simply switched off, and she went numb.

Her fellow cast members, not to mention the director, the dance choreographer, and assorted other people on whom the success of the play depended, still didn't give up hope. Over the months of working with Lena they had come to respect her and to care for her. They also recognized her talent and saw, too, that Lena was the type of personality who responded to gestures that were aimed directly at galvanizing that talent. In her dressing room in the Imperial Theatre on opening night, Lena heard a knock at the door. Outside the door was a huge bouquet of flowers with a card that read: "Savanna, we love you, The Crew." Immediately she snapped out of her autism and remembered that she was not in this mess alone—scores of people about whom she had come to care were depending on her to make *Jamaica* a success. As she took her place inside the little shack on stage that was Savanna's home, she remembered Robert Lewis's final words of advice: "Make your entrance like you belong there." "The entrance music stopped," she recalled in her autobiography, "I flung those shutters open hard and spoke clearly—like my grandmama taught me—barged down the steps, and stood still like Bobby had advised me—and New York treated me like a home-town girl . . . and I felt for the first time as if it were really me living on the Island, that I had been there always and that I did want to go to New York desperately."

Audiences and critics faulted the show for its weak story line, but few could resist its liveliness, its energy, the great Arlen

Harburg score, and Lena Horne, who, according to *Life*, "shines like a tigress in the night, purring and preening and pouncing into the spotlight and hurling herself into eight first-rate songs."

The show ran for over a year, closing in the spring of 1959. During those months Lena perfected her craft as an actress and learned to work a Broadway theater audience in much the same way she had earlier learned to work a cabaret audience. But the joy of appearing in *Jamaica* did not reside, for Lena, as much in the perfection of her craft as it did in the experience of joining together with other people. The cast, crew (many of whom were black, which made her proud), and other principals associated with *Jamaica* became a family to her—people to have over to dinner and for whom to bake sweet-potato pie, people whose moods she could assess and who could understand her moods, people she could fight with when she needed to fight, people who could count on her to be a willing combatant when a similar urge arose in them. Best of all, for Lena, was the opportunity to be settled in one place for a considerable length of time. She actually spent two Christmases in a row with her family. She actually formed friendships that she could count on maintaining in the same place and under consistent circumstances. *Jamaica* was not primarily a vehicle for her own success, but rather a means by which she was able to enjoy a style of life that she had yearned for from early childhood and never before been privileged to have.

10

LENA'S CIVIL RIGHTS MOVEMENT

AFTER *Jamaica* closed, Lena experienced a severe letdown, part of which was a natural response to having spent more than a year with the show and having arranged her life according to the Broadway schedule of evening performances and matinees. Suddenly there was nowhere she had to be at eight o'clock in the evening and two o'clock on Wednesday and Saturday afternoons. Moreover, doing *Jamaica* had fulfilled a long-held ambition, and now she had no similar goal toward which to strive.

She didn't want to go back into the clubs and sing about love and romance. Television was still not a viable medium for blacks in the United States. Broadway seemed brighter for blacks than it had in years—Lorraine Hansberry's *A Raisin in the Sun* had opened in 1958 and was among the most popular shows—but Lena received no offers that she cared to accept. For a time she was in a sort of limbo, going through the motions of resuming her career but failing to put her heart into it. She played The Sands in Las Vegas. She wrote a song with Sid Shaw called "If You Can't Afford the Punishment, Daddy, Please Don't Commit the Crime." She recorded the songs from *Porgy and Bess* on an album with

Harry Belafonte but was so displeased with the product that she went to court to try to stop its sale. Duets between Harry Belafonte and Lena Horne would seem surefire, but they hadn't actually sung any of the duets together. They had recorded their music separately, and then their voices had been united by RCA technicians. Lena charged that the result was so bad that it was "irreparably damaging to my career." The incident strained her relationship with both RCA and Belafonte, who thought the record sounded fine, but Lena was feeling strain in a lot of her relationships at the time. Months after the closing of *Jamaica* she was still feeling as if she didn't fit anywhere.

In the late summer she and Lennie went to Europe, where she appeared at a gala benefit in Monte Carlo on August 21, 1959, and at the London Savoy on September 21. They decided to get an apartment in Paris and just enjoy the city for a while. During their stay in Paris Lena received a letter from a writer named Richard Schickel who expressed interest in collaborating on her autobiography. He had approached a publisher with the idea, but the response had not been enthusiastic. As Lena told Art Buchwald, then Paris correspondent for the *Herald Tribune*, the publisher said, in effect, "As far as I know she's a dull broad and unless you can dig up some juicy scandal I don't know what you could do with it." Schickel still felt there would be a market for the book if Lena could come up with a gimmick; but Lena couldn't think of any gimmick. As she told Buchwald, "I haven't led a very interesting life."

Parts of Lena's life, even during this period of dissatisfaction, gave her pleasure. She was enjoying her long stay in Europe with Lennie and, at the same time, she had an opportunity to see Gail who, since graduating from Radcliffe in 1959, had been in Paris working for the magazine *Marie-Claire*. Gail would soon return to the United States and hold several different jobs—editing the guest newspaper at Grossinger's resort in the Catskills, working as a translator at Air France, and assisting in the production of an off-Broadway musical, *Miss Emily Adam*. She would gain a reputation for being one of the best-dressed young women in New

York, but that, she once told *Morning Telegraph* columnist Whitney Bolton, was almost inevitable: "My mother has a fetish. She will wear an evening gown only once. When I grew up enough to be able to wear her clothes, I inherited them all by default. I have, literally, never once bought an evening gown for myself." (Lena has always insisted she did it "for the women; they notice the clothes.") While at Radcliffe, Gail had played the lead in *School for Wives,* in Molière's own French, which won the Yale Drama Festival Award that year, and thus it came as no surprise to Lena when Gail played the ingenue lead in the off-Broadway musical, *Valmouth,* in the fall of 1960. Her vocal coach was Kay Thompson, who had coached Lena back in the early days at MGM and been a friend of the family ever since.

Teddy was doing well, too. He had moved to Los Angeles from Cleveland with his father and had attended Los Angeles High School, where he had been the first black to be elected president of the student body. From there he had gone to UCLA on a full, four-year scholarship. He was different from Gail in his political ideas—a conservative, while she was a staunch Democrat—but he, too, leaned toward the arts and wanted to become a writer. Lena worried that he would have a tough time.

While Lena felt good about her children and did accept some responsibility for their having turned out so well, she didn't feel good about herself. A sort of numbness had set into her soul, and she didn't recognize that her depression was a result of an unconscious attempt to suppress feelings of anger, which after years of conscious restraint, were welling up inside. An event with which she had nothing directly to do would soon serve to catalyze the feelings that she had long denied.

On February 1, 1960, a small group of students from the Negro Agricultural and Technical School in Greensboro, North Carolina, went to a Woolworth's in downtown Greensboro, took stools at the lunch counter, and ordered coffee. When they were refused service, they remained in their seats until the store closed. The next day they returned, now joined by some students from a nearby white college. Press coverage was extensive, and by the fourth day college students in neighboring states were following the Greensboro example. Thus began the student sit-in movement that spread across the South like a brushfire in the spring and summer of 1960 and the direct-action phase of the civil rights movement.

Lena's reaction was immediate and passionate. She *felt* for those students and the torment they went through, sitting quietly day after day while racists shouted epithets at them, until the police came, picked them up bodily, and hauled them off to jail. "I felt so bad and so pained. I knew I was awake again," she told Ponchitta Pierce in an interview for *Ebony* eight years later. "I wasn't just reacting automatically. I had been dead for so long but those students made me live again." Initially, she had no idea how to channel her new feelings. She had no intention of heading South to join the movement. The students were a new generation, and she suspected that they did not hold her in very high regard. After all, her generation had practiced moderation, minded their manners, presented relatively few challenges to the status quo. The more progressive among them had been content to function as symbols, to show the white majority by sterling example that blacks were worthy of equality. Comparing her efforts to be "a credit to her race" to the action of the Southern students, Lena felt a sense of anger and shame.

On February 17, 1960, Lena sat alone at a table in the Luau Restaurant in Beverly Hills. She and Lennie had arranged to meet Kay Thompson there at midnight, and when Kay didn't show up Lennie went to find a telephone to call her. As Lena recalled, a drunk at an adjoining table began to demand immediate service from the waiter who was on his way to Lena's table with a tray of drinks. When informed that the waiter had to serve "Miss Horne's table" first, the man yelled, "So what? She's just another nigger. Where is she?" Lena jumped up, cried, "Here I am, you bastard!" and let fly with every object within reach, including a lamp, glasses, and a conch-shell ashtray that hit its mark. The manager of the restaurant later observed that a bamboo divider and a ship model that separated the two tables probably hampered Lena's

150

aim and saved her victim from being hurt more seriously. The manager and a waiter immediately hustled away Harvey St. Vincent, who was bleeding profusely from a cut over his eyebrow. Meanwhile, Lennie had returned. Grabbing Lena from behind, he said, "What happened?" When Lena told him, he asked simply, "Did you hit him?" St. Vincent insisted at first that he had made no racist remarks, and the reporter who happened to be in the restaurant when the incident occurred duly recorded his statements. But apparently many people who heard about it and read about it in the morning paper believed otherwise.

Lena and Lennie left the restaurant almost immediately after St. Vincent had been taken away. Lena just wanted to go home and go to bed. The next morning the press arrived, which she had expected. Completely unexpected were the telephone calls and telegrams and, later, the letters from black people congratulating her, many of which were written before St. Vincent admitted that he had indeed made the remark of which Lena had accused him. As Lena told Ponchitta Pierce, "I can't tell you what a shock that was to me because I didn't think anybody cared. . . . I had lost sight of the fact that I had ties with my own people. I told Lennie, 'But I always get mad, this isn't the first time I've had a fight because of some insult from a white person.' But it was the first time it happened when a newspaperman was right there and the guy was pretty bloody. Lennie said, 'Well, darling, I guess maybe your people just don't know you feel that way.' Then I realized how important it was that they do. I don't know whether it was important to them but I knew it was for me. . . . It was the first sign of identification that I felt. I had always been militant and I got angry like a lot of other black people. But it was never in any place that anybody knew about because I was completely in that white world reacting as a black woman."

One of Lena's first actions, after coming to what she felt was a profound realization about herself, was to contact Richard Schickel, the writer who had approached her about doing her autobiography. She suddenly felt that she had something important to say and, over the next months, she found that speaking about her life into a tape recorder helped her to review her past in terms of her present revelation. She realized that there had been an aridity about her years as a performer in a white world, a deliberate attempt at steely control so that she would be accepted by whites while retaining a modicum of dignity. She had spoken up, certainly, but she had spoken up for herself and for her family, not for her people. As she had told Art Buchwald less than two months earlier, "I can't get up in a nightclub in a $1,000 dress and start singing 'Let My People Go.'" She hadn't identified with blacks as *her* people and hadn't felt that they identified with her as other than a symbol, and so she had felt no compelling reason to speak out on their behalf. Being a symbol had seemed enough to her.

Lena did not reveal the changes that were going on inside her in her outward actions or statements for a while. She attended to business as usual, doing selected club dates and a few recordings. She was doing more television—the usual variety shows like Perry Como's, the host she liked best because he had always treated her like a human being and had refused to obey the unspoken taboo against touching between whites and blacks before the TV cameras; plus an occasional role in a dramatic series. She would have liked to do more, particularly a special, but finding a negative reception in the United States—the first series featuring a black entertainer, "The Bill Cosby Show," would not air until 1970—she went to London to do the television work that was denied her in her own country.

Back in New York, she appeared in an Alexander H. Cohen production called *Lena Horne in Her Nine O'Clock Revue*, an after-dinner theater presentation that featured, in addition to Lena, comedian Don Adams, dance couple Augie and Margo, and the singing group the Delta Rhythm Boys.

Under an assumed name, she and Lennie had purchased a house in Palm Springs in the late 1950s; they went there often. She returned annually to Monte Carlo for its Sporting Club International Gala and continued her work with the NAACP and other organizations with which she had long been affiliated, as well as with Delta Sigma Theta, a national black women's service sorority, in which she was a relatively new, honorary member.

During the run of *Jamaica,* Jean Noble, president of that sorority, sent Lena several letters, but Lena had never read them. Over the years, and since she had hired a secretary, she had become accustomed to not reading her mail. Partly, this was due to the fact that she was too busy to read it all; partly, too, she had sought protection from the hate mail that regularly arrived. The people whom she employed to take care of such matters as her correspondence brought to her attention all the myriad requests for financial support or benefit performances. But each time she heard the word *sorority* she dismissed the correspondence from Delta out of hand. In her mind, sororities were frivolous groups and a waste of time. Finally, Noble had gone to the Imperial Theatre to find Lena and persuade her that DST was not at all frivolous. Its members were all black women with college degrees, and its projects ranged from voter-registration drives to raising funds for scholarships. Impressed by Jean Noble and the work of Delta, Lena happily accepted honorary membership, and during the time when she was struggling with her identity as a black person and trying to fit herself at least mentally into the civil rights movement, her contact with Delta was comforting to her. As she said in her autobiography, "Its activities seemed to me ones that I could, given my age and the sort of life I lived, appropriately take part in."

While she felt energetic and very much alive since coming out of the numbing apathy that had descended upon her after *Jamaica* closed, Lena remained keenly aware that she was part of a generation that the young movers and shakers of the direct-action civil rights struggle did not respect. She watched as older leaders took steps to channel the energy of the militant college students—the formation of the Southern Christian Leadership Conference; the rise to national prominence of the Reverend Martin Luther King, Jr., who had directed the successful Montgomery bus boycott in

1955-56; the control that King had taken over the direction of the movement in the South. But she still did not feel that the movement would welcome her. King was ten years younger than she, his name not sullied by a prior history of accommodationism. There was just no way she could join the avant-garde of the movement unscathed. She regretted the bad timing, for she longed to prove her growing reidentification with her people by doing something significant in the civil rights cause.

Yet when she did have the opportunity to do something significant, she backed out. In the spring of 1963, King and others in the SCLC, in association with the Student Nonviolent Coordinating Committee (SNCC) and other civil rights groups, launched a campaign in Birmingham, Alabama. Members of Delta planned to participate in some of the marches and Lena was invited to sing on the steps of a Birmingham church during a Mother's Day march. Lena was in Palm Springs when she was contacted by Delta, who wanted her to fly East to join them for the trip to Birmingham. Lena begged off, explaining that she was afraid to fly. She had never liked flying and during the war years and in the fifties she had been involved in so many near-crashes that she had refused to board a plane since. One suspects, however, that if Lena had really been committed to marching in Birmingham she would have traveled by hot-air balloon if necessary, and that the real problem was that her militancy was still a mental attitude rather than a disposition to act. She was angry with herself, and while the fact that the Deltas had not, after all, participated in the Birmingham march because of the possibility of violence helped her to justify to some extent her refusal to take part, a substantial feeling of guilt remained over the fact that she had not, at a critical time, been able to act.

The violence in Birmingham catalyzed the Kennedy administration to action of sorts. Attorney General Robert F. Kennedy decided to meet with a select group of prominent blacks, and writer James Baldwin asked Lena to participate. Although Lena didn't know what she could contribute to the meeting, she

154

allowed Lennie to persuade her to go, and to go by plane, for, as he explained to her, if she didn't go she would hate herself, and then, quite possibly, she would also begin to hate him.

The principals at the meeting, which was held in New York, included Robert F. Kennedy and his aide, Burke Marshall; the actor Rip Torn, a Southerner and a friend of Baldwin's; sociologists Dr. Kenneth Clark and Dr. Brewton Berry; the playwright Lorraine Hansberry; Harry Belafonte; and Jerome Smith, a young man from SNCC. Lena recalls that they sat around quoting statistics and mouthing platitudes until Jerome Smith decided it was time to cut through the bull. His passionate recitation of the beatings and jailings to which he and other SNCC voter-registration workers had been subjected in the South, his fury, and his plain talk awakened the anger and the alienation of all the other blacks in the room, and Attorney General Kennedy learned just what they thought about well-meaning Northerners who continued to support the economy of a region whose social policies were supposedly anathema to them.

Lena left the meeting feeling that little had been accomplished but inspired to go South and do whatever she could to help. She called the NAACP and learned that there was to be a rally in Jackson, Mississippi, at which she could sing. She asked Jean Noble and her son, Teddy, whose work with civil rights groups she could point to in the absence of credentials of her own, to go with her, and she asked Billy Strayhorn to be her accompanist.

On arrival in Jackson, Lena's party was met by Medgar Evers, director of the NAACP Field Office in Jackson. Lena was immediately impressed with Evers, who was managing to control a potentially volatile situation in Jackson. More militant workers and the comedian Dick Gregory were in favor of a march through Jackson, but Evers had been directed to confine the activity to the rally. Gregory charged that the NAACP was more concerned with Lena's safety than with the rights of the blacks in Jackson, and Lena hated to be the focus of conflict between the two men. She was not particularly concerned, she says, with what the whites in the area might do; she was far more worried about how she would be received by the blacks, and she was relieved and gratified when the ordinary blacks who attended the rally welcomed her warmly.

Not only did Lena sing at the rally, she also gave her first bona fide civil rights speech:

> The battle that you are fighting here in Jackson, and the battle that you are fighting in other cities of the South, is this nation's Number One crisis. It *is* the crisis. And let it be understood that your courage, and your grim determination—the determination of all these Negroes in this fight down here in these Southern cities—let me tell you, they've challenged and triggered the battle that's gonna flame the whole nation.
>
> You all know that I work in the theater, and I raise money in certain ways. A lot of us have to use a great many means to get the purpose taken care of. And I want to say that it's no hardship because we've all got to do it. And no Negro, in fact nobody black or white who really believes in democracy can stand aside now, *everybody's* got to stand up and be counted.
>
> I have a son—he's here with me tonight. I'm very proud of him. He works on the West Coast. He goes to school out there, but he works with CORE, with SNCC—with young people because he is young. He's doing part of my battle—in fact, a great deal of it—and I'm very proud to have a son like that. You see, I can't—and I know you can't—look at what happened to that man at that lunch counter here, and I can't look at what happened to that woman that had those cops kneeling on her neck, and *I* can't look at those children sitting along the water, and I can't look at all that and not know that I don't want my *child's* child to have to take this.

Warmed by the welcome she'd received in Jackson, and awed by the character of Medgar Evers, Lena was eager to do more on behalf of the movement. She thus accepted an invitation from Hugh Downs to appear on the "Today Show." She went to bed early the night before and was at the studio in the RCA Building by six o'clock the next morning. Waiting for her call to go on the show, she was informed that there would be a delay because they were waiting for Roy Wilkins, Executive Director of the NAACP. Then she learned that Medgar Evers had been assassinated the night before. Though shaken, Lena went on the show with Wilkins and tried to explain what Medgar Evers had stood for. His death caused Lena to be even more determined to assist the movement in any way she could.

She went to Atlanta, Georgia, to sing at an SCLC rally. She participated in the March on Washington in August. She did an article for *Show* magazine on what it was like to be black—"I Just Want to Be Myself"—and found that it did indeed have an impact. Harold Arlen read it and decided that songwriters like himself should make some contribution to the movement. So he dusted off a piece he had written originally with Ira Gershwin, and Yip Harburg put new, more contemporary lyrics to it, and the result was a song that Lena felt she could sing. It was called "Silent Spring," and it was dedicated to the memory of the four little children who died in the bombing of the Sixteenth Street Baptist Church in Birmingham on September 15, 1963. Lena also persuaded Arlen to accompany her in a medley of songs, including "Silent Spring," at an upcoming benefit for SNCC at Carnegie Hall.

Another song was specially written for her to sing at that benefit. Adolph Green and Betty Comden put some biting and angry lyrics to the Jewish tune "Hava Nagillah" and called it "Now," and on the night of the benefit Lena sang it with all the fervor she had been unable to summon for her traditional repertoire. Bud Granoff, a producer at Twentieth Century-Fox records, was at the benefit that night, and he asked her to record the song. By late October it had gone out to radio disc jockeys and a considerable furor resulted. In Los Angeles, seven out of eleven stations banned it, some station spokesmen saying it was because the record was "pretty strong integration advocacy," some insisting that it simply didn't fit in with the style of music they ordinarily played. In New York, by contrast, only WCBS banned the record, citing its policy against "rock 'n' roll, 'screamers,' or 'wailers'" Hearing that, Lena laughed, "I think it's marvelous to be

157

classified with the wailers. They are the ones that sell all the records." All ten other stations did play it. At WNEW, disc jockey William B. Williams asked the listeners to call in with their opinions after he played it. "The calls came in fifteen to one in favor of the record," Williams told Mort Young of the *New York Journal-American*. "It's a musically exciting record. Lena obviously felt deeply about what she was singing. I'm airing it as often as possible. I'm just wondering if it'll be played in Birmingham." Bud Granoff claimed that 185,000 of the records were sold in the first three days of its release, and Lena, who had never had a hit record, was "flabbergasted." She decided to donate part of the proceeds from sales of the record to civil rights organizations.

Her daughter Gail married director Sidney Lumet on November 23, 1963, and Lena, Lennie, and Teddy all attended the wedding. Lena insisted that her only regret was that she was losing her daughter after just getting a chance to know her as an adult. Gail had stayed at 300 West End Avenue after returning to New York from Paris, and it was the first time mother and daughter had been together for an extended time since Gail was a baby. Lena could hardly object to her daughter's marriage on the grounds that Sidney Lumet was white—she was the third generation of Horne women to marry white men—but she may have wished privately that Gail had somehow signified that she was part of a new generation by marrying within her own race. Also, at thirty-nine, Sidney was fourteen years older than Gail and had already been married twice.

While Lena continued to devote much of her time to singing at benefits for various civil rights organizations and otherwise helping the movement, and to reading as much as she could about the history of black civil rights struggles in the United States, by late 1963 she began to feel eager to return to her career again. She had another long-held ambition for which she now felt capable of striving—to have her own U.S. television special—and in late March of 1964 she and Lennie set out for England to attract the necessary backing. England's Associated Television had already produced three specials for her in Britain and were quite willing to support a fourth. Accordingly, she and Lennie went to work preparing the material. The special aired in England in early November, and immediately afterward Independent Television went after the U.S. market. By mid-December the company had sold the special to thirty-five markets, including New York; Los Angeles; Decatur, Illinois; and Peoria, Illinois—and if it would play in Peoria. . . .

The special aired in late December and was very much devoted to Lena. Her one guest was James Mason, a long-time friend, whose relatives had made Lena and Lennie feel welcome during their first visit to England back in 1947. Except for the numbers that they sang together, Lena sang only solos, and interspersed them with reminiscences about her career that the reviewer for the *New York Herald Tribune* found irritating: "The chit-chat about Miss Horne's career, however, was a mistake intruding on the entertainment. It was as slight and inconclusive as a family joke. . . . And it gave this otherwise fine sing-along the faint flavor of a retrospective of Miss Horne's vocalizing. The last thing her audience wants is a farewell concert. What Miss Horne needs is more TV work."

More was in the offing, and Lena happily accepted all the invitations she received to do television in the United States—a January 19 "Bell Telephone Hour," another appearance on the "Ed Sullivan Show," another on Perry Como's. Meanwhile, she was working hard to finish tape-recording the rest of her auto-biography in advance of the early 1965 deadline for submission of the completed manuscript, but she was finding that her words were flowing more easily now.

She believed that she had finally achieved a real sense of her own identity, had become a "whole person" at last. She had discovered herself as a black person, had been able to identify with her people, and in the process she had also been able to draw together most of the pieces of her fragmented life. In an epilogue to her autobiography she rejoiced in the birth in November 1964 of Gail's first child, Amy Lumet. She had gone to be with her daughter in England for the birth, and ironically the delivery was both long and difficult, as Lena's first delivery had been. She rejoiced, too, in the reestablishment of her ties with her father, communication with whom had lapsed over the years, even after he had accepted her marriage to Lennie and even after she had bought a small hotel in Las Vegas and asked him to manage it. As she related, one day she picked up the telphone and called him in Las Vegas and told him, for the first time, that she loved him. She ended her story on a very upbeat note, choosing, as was her right, not to admit that there were still some problems she hadn't quite worked out.

While she felt close to Gail and saw, in the infant Amy, evidence of a kind of historic, family thread, she still had not achieved the closeness with her son that she desired. Teddy had already made her a grandmother, having fathered twin sons, but she didn't feel that he considered her a part of his family. Also, she despaired of ever establishing a real sense of closeness with her mother. The inner conflict she had experienced over Gail's marriage had caused her to believe that it was essential that she work out the love-hate problem with her own mother, Edna. Gail kept telling her that she couldn't understand Gail's feelings because she, Lena, had never had a real mother. Lena tried, but unfortunately Edna Rodriguez was too bitter to respond in the way Lena hoped she would. Many years later, Lena told Marie Brenner of *New York* magazine about her futile attempts to resolve her relationship with Edna: "I went to see her and I said, 'Mommy, do you love me?' and she said, 'No.' I just broke down. 'Lena, I wanted a career,' she told me. 'I wanted what you have. I wanted to be glamorous. I wanted to be famous.' I asked her, 'Why did you have me?' and she said, 'I only married your father because he was the best-looking guy in our set. We wanted a boy and we got you and you got my career.'

"'Mommy,' I told her, 'I didn't want the career. I never wanted to be a singer. I only wanted you to love me. I would give you every bit of it if I could. You could have had all of it, if only I thought you cared about me.' My mother looked at me and said, 'It's over now, Lena. Just forget about it.'"

Lena also chose not to share with the readers of her autobiography the fact that her feelings for Lennie had changed since her new awakening. During the time when she became active in the civil rights movement, the experience of being taken so easily into the hearts of ordinary blacks caused her to recoil from the liberal whites to whom she had always before been so grateful for acceptance. She saw herself in an adversary position to whites, and it irritated her when Lennie continued not to see her as a black woman, particularly when, her senses now so keenly sharpened to her own blackness, she began to see him as a white man. This was no doubt uncomfortable for Lennie, given that over the years he had come to think as a black in many ways. It was a natural development, since marriage to Lena exposed him to discrimination and caused him to become sensitive to racial inequality, and he was taken aback when the sensitivity that Lena, and their situation, had demanded of him over the years was suddenly not enough. After all the years they had been together, and all the experiences they had been through together, a great chasm of experience and attitude suddenly divided them. Lena felt that gap most keenly when Malcolm X was assassinated in February 1965. She had met Malcolm only once, back in Harlem years before, when he had not yet taken his Muslim name; but she had read his autobiography and held him in high esteem for having grown so much as a person. When he was assassinated she was devastated, and she was similarly devastated at Lennie's reaction. Years later she told Gil Noble on the TV program "Like It Is": "The day Malcolm was killed, my husband said, 'Oh, those rabblerousers always kill each other,' and I turned and left. I couldn't believe that someone who'd known me for twenty-odd years could say something like that. But then, you don't know people; it takes a long while to know people."

Lena decided that she couldn't be with her husband at that time and still retain what was good about their relationship. She still loved him and needed him, and because she wanted to continue loving and needing him she believed that they had to be apart for a while. As she told Ponchitta Pierce in 1968:

> I took a chance. I said, "Lennie, I'm going through some changes as a black woman. I can't explain them. I don't know what they're going to mean, what they're going to do to me, but I've got to be by myself to work it out—to think about it." And believe it or not, he had to make a very big change himself. He had been working with me, we had built a little ivory tower where we had traveled together, we were together every minute, our social life, what little of it, after work, our daytime activities, sleep, eat, rehearse, work. He had to go back into a profession he had left, back to conducting and writing for movies. . . .

Lennie returned to the West Coast. There, he got involved in arranging for television, which by this time was centered in the Hollywood area, and worked on shows for "Chrysler Theater," "Voyage to the Bottom of the Sea," "The Virginian," and "Daniel Boone," among others. Twentieth Century-Fox asked him to score its movie, *Star*, a film biography of Gertrude Lawrence. He then worked on the film version of *Hello, Dolly* and won an Academy Award for it in 1970. Lena remained in New York, working for the civil rights cause. Although they saw each other occasionally, they lived apart for about three years.

11

TRIPLE
TRAGEDY

LENA, the autobiography written with Richard Schickel, was published by Doubleday in the fall of 1965, and between October 18 and November 18 Lena went on an autographing tour that covered twelve cities. She was most successful in Detroit where, at Hudson's department store on November 3, she autographed five hundred copies in two hours. Lengthy excerpts from the book were run in several periodicals, and Lena was pleased to be able to further the cause of the civil rights movement by sharing her experiences as a black in a racist society. When she was contacted by the National Council for Negro Women (NCNW), who wanted her to use the book as the basis for a panel-discussion tour in a series of Northern and Southern cities, she was skeptical about the likely success of such an idea but willing to try. She was amazed to find the discussions very well attended by middle-class black women and to hear the feelings of those women. She learned, in the course of the tour, that "we privileged Negro women not only share common problems but today we face a three-horned 'dilemma.' First there is that hideous word 'matriarchy' and all it means in our relationships with Negro men. Secondly, we have a score to settle with two-fifths of our sex, the so-called 'indigenous poor' Negro women. And thirdly, there is a need for redefining relationships with the liberal white women who had traditionally been identified with our cause." She shared her feelings about these concerns as she traveled around the country and wrote about them in an article for *Ebony* with the help of Jean Noble, president of Delta Sigma Theta.

Thereafter, Lena added the NCNW to the list of organizations that she actively supported and became involved in their efforts to address that "three-horned dilemma." With a $300,000 grant from the Ford Foundation, the NCNW undertook an ambitious project to train and upgrade the status of domestics, and Lena took the responsibility of organizing a giant benefit for domestic cooperatives. Lena and the NCNW also took steps to strengthen their ties with white women's service organizations. As to bettering relations between black women and black men, the NCNW confined itself to urging, in speeches and panel discussions, more understanding of their men by black women. Lena spoke often on the subject and expressed regret that she had not been more supportive of her first husband. Through these and other activities Lena believed that she was indeed managing to "salvage something constructive" from her traditional glamorous image.

What Lena especially enjoyed about her work with the NCNW and other black organizations was her opportunity to be with "her people," and when she wasn't working on various service projects she sought out black friends with whom to spend her time. One of the oldest and closest was Elois Davis, whose late husband had been black Hollywood's "doctor to the stars," having treated Nat "King" Cole, Cab Calloway, Billie Holiday, and many others besides Lena. Dalili Davis, Elois's daughter-in-law, recalls a summer then when Lena, who had purchased a house around the corner from the Davis home, spent several weeks there. "I had to lug blackeye peas back and forth between the two soul sisters," Davis recalls, "and once in a while I had to go get my mother-in-law, and I'd find them having a drink and a knock-down, drag-out conversation." Davis remembers seeing Lennie on occasion and hearing Lena and Lennie talk about music and Lena's latest album, about which she was very excited. "They were almost like brother and sister," says Davis. "I knew that they maintained separate residences, but I did not inquire into their personal lives. They seemed to understand each other."

Lena's father became ill with emphysema during this time, and he was forced to give up the operation of the hotel in Las Vegas. Lena persuaded him to move to the house near the Davis's and to live with her. At last, he allowed her to get close to him, and they enjoyed the relationship that she had always wanted but couldn't have. "We were like brother and sister, like husband and wife," she told John Gruen of *Vogue* in 1972.

Lena's father had left her when she was three years old, just at the time when a child begins, in Freudian theory, to feel attracted to the parent of the opposite sex. Deprived of that normal stage of psychological development, a child can spend decades unconsciously searching for that absent, opposite-sex parent. Lena has said that when she married Louis Jones she was actually marrying her father. Later, after she married Lennie, she was in the habit of calling him "Daddy," although when asked why she insisted that it was nothing Freudian: she had started dating Lennie when her children were small, she explained, and had told them they might have a new daddy. Lena is a well-read and highly intelligent woman, and no doubt she had read extensively on the subject of parent identification and tried hard to resolve the need she recognized in herself. Still, looking back a couple of years after her father's death, to their time together in Los Angeles and speaking off-the-cuff to an interviewer, she had compared their relationship to that of "husband and wife." "She could cook for him and care for him," Dalili Davis recalls. "She worshipped her father. Any time she was out of town—while she was on tours and things—she'd be calling my mother-in-law regularly to find out how he was doing, did he need this, did he need that. She spent a lot of energy trying to see that he was comfortable." She could talk to him about things that even she and Lennie couldn't talk about. "*Our* thing was there," Lena says, "and had always been there."

Teddy would come by to visit, and the times when the three of them were together were joyous times for Lena. "The three of us had this great new thing. We'd discuss the hustles of our lives. It was all for the first time. And I belonged! I belonged to *them*! I belonged to my people."

Sadly, the joy for all of them was bittersweet. They didn't have much time. Teddy Horne was seriously debilitated by emphysema and could not be expected to live many more years. More tragic than the impending death of this elderly man, who had lived his life without apologizing to anyone for it, was the illness of young Teddy, who had been diagnosed as having an incurable kidney disease at the age of twenty-one, when he was still at UCLA. While Lena refused to recognize the fact that he, too, did not have long to live, a twinge of sadness crept into her heart every once in a while and lodged there in the moments before she stubbornly willed it away.

Around 1967, Lena gave up the apartment at 300 West End Avenue and moved into a small apartment in the East 90s, just a few blocks away from Gail and Sidney's four-story brownstone on East 91st. When she was there, and not on the Coast, she also made a point of gathering family and black friends around her. Dalili Davis and her husband were living in New York at the time, and Davis remembers spending a Thanksgiving there. "She had two uncles there with her. One was a poet [Frank Horne], and I remember him reciting some poetry. There was a book with some of his works in it, and I remember him talking about the Harlem Renaissance era. The other, much younger [Burke Horne], was manager of the Apollo Theatre. I remember riding up there in a car with Lena, and she was very casual and people didn't pay any attention to her—maybe because of the way she carried herself they didn't think she was anybody special. I think she enjoyed going around incognito. From then on, I used to be able to get into the shows at the Apollo because I knew Lena's uncle. There was a great warmth, a great sense of family between them, and I enjoyed that feeling."

In 1967 Lena Horne turned fifty. When she was thirty, Duke Ellington said, "Well, there's the rose, full bloom and everything." When she was fifty, he shook his head and said, "There's the bud." Lena Horne at fifty was just beginning to blossom. In a way, she felt apologetic about it—"I'm a late bloomer," she would explain. She was not talking about her looks, but just about everyone else was. From the time she was forty, interviewers had started asking her how she kept her looks, what were her beauty secrets, and by her fiftieth birthday these questions seemed to take precedence over all others. She had no special beauty regimen, she insisted—she did not exercise regularly, hated to swim. Lennie had bought her a bicycle, but she didn't ride it very often; about every two months she lay down and did fifty bicycle pumps. People began to investigate how old she really was. Lena dismissed all the interest in her physical appearance as foolishness. *She* was much more concerned with blooming as a person. "I feel young," she explained. "That's an unusual feeling for me: I was always so old inside."

By the time she turned fifty she had discovered much about herself and had resolved many of the conflicts that had plagued her. She had reestablished the relationship with her father that had been cut off when she was just a child; she had come to know her son better. She had accepted her daughter as a person in her own right. She had come to know and feel part of her people. Having accomplished all that, she felt able to return to Lennie about 1960 and to reestablish their relationship on a basis that was much stronger than it had been before.

For Lena at fifty, *strength* was the word. Asked how she had managed to stay so youthful-looking, she answered, "strong stock." Asked how she felt about the continuing racial problems in the country, despite the gains made by the civil rights movement, she answered, "I find strength because I'm black. I just think if I were white in these days . . . I think I couldn't survive if I were like those people. I feel I have more at stake in life than they do. . . . The stake is that I'd want a black woman who now is 30 years younger than I to miss all that crap, or a man at the age of my son to be able to be free and not as hung up. I still have that faith."

In fact she had never felt so strong, and thus when Martin Luther King, Jr. was assassinated in April 1968 she didn't feel as if her world had come apart. Instead, she felt angry—angry at whites for their arrogance, for their assumption that it was their right to spoil things, angry because, with the death of Martin Luther King, Jr., she felt that she would have to readjust her hopes and consider the idea that "in my time and even in my children's time I'm not going to see much more." For Lena, the assassination of King meant the end of the inexorable and consistent drive for black progress; King's memory would live on, but what about his leadership? Her anger blotted out Lennie, and she attended King's funeral in Atlanta without him, wanting to be alone in her grief. Later she realized that her husband's grief had been as deep as hers and she apologized for not having been able to share it. Part of her wished he had been there with her at the funeral, but part of her was also relieved that he had not accompanied her, for she believed that the other black people at the funeral might have felt uncomfortable. Lennie, as always, understood.

During the time when Lena was actively involved in the civil rights movement and in her work with Delta and the NCNW, she had curtailed her performing career. While she had continued to record an occasional album, and to play a few selected club dates, most of her performing had been at benefits. She had not played Las Vegas or Reno since 1966, having developed what she described as an allergic reaction to air conditioning as well as to the glue used to affix her false eyelashes. She had been offered a role in *Hallelujah, Baby!* on Broadway but had turned it down because she considered it old-fashioned and full of clichés. Nor did she feel she owed that much to the writers Adolph Green and Betty Comden just because they had written the words to her controversial and highly successful recording of "Now." Leslie Uggams got the role in the musical, which opened in April 1967. Thus it came as a complete surprise when Universal approached her to play a movie role. She hadn't made a picture since *Meet Me in Las Vegas* (1956), and she hadn't had a speaking role, which she was being offered now, since *Stormy Weather.*

Her first reaction was to decline the offer. Then she read the script and got to thinking about it. Called *Patch,* the screenplay was based on the novel *Patch's Law* by Lewis B. Patten and centered around a marshall in a small Western town who is in danger of losing his job because of the encroachment of civilization. Having killed his thirteenth man, he is criticized by local businessmen for scaring away Eastern money; but the real reason may be that he has been around long enough to know too much about them. A substantial subplot is Patch's love for the operator of one of the two local houses of prostitution, which vie with one another for preeminence, and Lena was asked to play the character of this frontier madam.

She saw that the script made no reference at all to race. She was told that Jennings Lang, senior vice-president at Universal, had suggested her. After seeing her on a Dean Martin television show, he'd called her "the most attractive lady who is mature—of any color." She realized that at long last she was being asked to play a role in an intelligent movie that didn't depend in any way on stereotypes or clichés. She took the role.

Lena reported to work on *Patch* on June 1, 1968, armed with her acting coach and an outward determination to do well that she did not feel inside. She was an entertainer, not an actress, and since accepting the role she had gone through weeks of self-doubt. Sidney Lumet, her son-in-law, had advised her, "Be simple, be still, don't act," yet she had found herself pacing the floor every night and throwing up every morning (a physical reaction usually reserved for the times when she was so angry she couldn't control herself). She had even done some research on houses of ill-repute in small Western towns, for it had struck her as odd that such a small town would have had two such houses; she learned that a two-house town was fairly tame compared to other towns. Unfortunately, that research had not made her more confident about playing the role of a madam. Having studied the script

169

intently, she had a flip answer when she was asked by reporters how she felt about her first serious acting role in many years: "Just wind me up and point me and I'll say 'Frank'" (the first word she was to say, according to the script).

Wayne Warga of the *Los Angeles Times* found her in the Universal commissary so busy ogling other stars that she didn't notice that she herself was the center of attention. Joan Barthel of *The New York Times* found her on location near Hollywood after a morning's work in the dust of the Western movie set. Lena arrived for the interview fresh and dry and explaining, "I saw those other people not sweatin' so I decided not to let my culture show." She then looked at the milk on the lunch tray that had been brought to her and wished she'd had some iced tea. Wrote Barthel in her article, "Can you believe it doesn't occur to her that a movie star need only mention?"

After lunch, Lena dissected her morning's performance: "I sounded like an ass. I don't like saying lines outdoors. Maybe if they'd stand me up against a post I could sing them."

Lena was not exhibiting false modesty. One of the nice things about being fifty-one years old was that she didn't feel she had anything to prove—any image to project. She was as honestly insecure about playing opposite Richard Widmark in *Patch* as she'd been about playing opposite Ricardo Montalban in *Jamaica* on Broadway. She'd always been nervous when she had stepped outside the medium of singing, but in the distant past she had worried about messing up because of her position as a symbol; by the time she reached the age of forty, with *Jamaica*, she had worried more about her effect on the product, and on her co-workers. And she worried, now, about the effect of her acting on *Patch*.

Retitled *Death of a Gunfighter*, the movie was released in the spring of 1969 and received excellent critical reviews, although despite a vigorous publicity campaign it was not the box-office success that Universal had hoped. Lena's character, according to the *Los Angeles Times* reviewer, was only one of a large number of well-observed, peripheral characters, but she gave an admirable performance. The more cynical *Variety* review read in part, "Miss

Horne, first as Widmark's mistress, then his wife, is in obviously for name value only, for her footage is comparatively brief. She sings one song, 'Sweet Apple Wine,' over opening credits and finale." Neither review mentioned that the movie featured an interracial love affair.

Lena's appearance in the film heralded no new Hollywood career for her. There weren't many roles available for a "mature woman," and the explosion of black films that would mark the early 1970s would, in their glorification of poverty and the ghetto, exploit a militance with which Lena, even at her most angry, could never be identified.

Lena turned her attention back to television as soon as she completed filming *Death of a Gunfighter*. In August 1968 she did a special in Canada that Harry Belafonte produced, the strain in their relationship over the *Porgy and Bess* album having long been forgotten in their mutual eagerness to support the civil rights movement. "I don't even ask for TV anymore here," she told an interviewer for *The New York Times*. "If they want to shape up, let them prove it to me; I'm through trying to prove something to them." The following year "they" did shape up, and in September 1969 NBC broadcast "Monsanto Night Presents Lena Horne," her first American special.

Months of planning went into the project. Discussions about guest stars were particularly important, for Lena wanted guests who would fit into the relaxed, spontaneous atmosphere that would mark the show. O. C. Smith, who had a hit recording called "God Didn't Make Little Green Apples," had worked with Count Basie for several years and "really knew his stuff," in Lena's opinion. Ralph Harris, who was executive producer on the show, suggested David Janssen, star of the TV series "The Fugitive," and Lena immediately concurred: "David and I have the kind of relaxed, easy rapport that comes from a long-time friendship," she told Bill Pollack of the *Los Angeles Herald-Examiner*. "This is David's first experience in a musical. It's exciting to see someone do well in something new." A young vocal group called The Honeycones and a folk/jazz guitarist, Gabor Szabo, completed the guest list.

171

Taping was done in July. Lena opened the show with "Watch What Happens," followed by "A Flower Is a Lovesome Thing," a gentle ballad written by Billy Strayhorn, who had recently died, and arranged by Lennie. But the majority of the dozen other solos Lena sang were contemporary—direct and honest—a Beatles song "Blackbird," a song from *Hair*, "Turning Point." She sang Jimmy Webb's "Didn't We" with O. C. Smith, "I Remember It Well" with Janssen, danced in an exotic number with six male dancers, all dressed in black unisex Nehru-look pantsuits, and performed with The Honeycones in a simulated rehearsal scene. Only three of her songs were from her traditional repertoire: "Surrey with the Fringe on Top," "Stormy Weather," and "Hello, Young Lovers."

When Lena's first American special aired she was on the stage at Caesar's Palace in Las Vegas with Harry Belafonte. It was the first time she had played Las Vegas since 1966. "I wouldn't even be doing it at Caesar's if it weren't for Harry," she insisted. "We've done so many benefits and we're such close friends that it was sort of an 'I will if you will' thing. Other than that, who needs it?" Their show at Caesar's was so well received—one reviewer wrote, "Together, their lyrics and voices blend, as if telling an exquisite love story"—that they did a television special, sponsored by Fabergé, on ABC in March 1970, their only appearance on TV together, except for a stint on "The Tonight Show" in 1967. Even Lena was impressed with the turnaround by American television that would allow her to do two specials in the space of six months, and would see the second actually nominated for an Emmy.

A few months later Lena's father died. He had been ill for years, and Lena had been expecting it. She had made her peace with him, had managed to enjoy, for a brief time, the closeness with him that she had missed for most of her life. He, too, had made his peace with his own life, and as he lay dying he was able to think of Lena and to give her comfort. "When my father was dying, I sat with him a long time," she told John Gruen of *Vogue*. "He was very gentle with me. I think he was getting me ready for Teddy's death."

Teddy's death was also expected, although Lena had never been able to accept its inevitability. He was such a bright, sensitive young man. After completing his undergraduate work at UCLA, he had gone to UCLA Law School, also on a full scholarship, and since receiving his degree had worked in the Watts Labor Communication Center, taught classes in Spanish, devoted his life to helping the unfortunate people who didn't want anything very extraordinary out of life but who were denied even the simple things. Lena was immensely proud of him and unable to accept the idea that he could not be cured. To her, it seemed simply too unfair, for he was "a potentially great man. . . . People like Ted are needed to help make up for the loss of our princes," she said in 1968. "Malcolm is gone and Martin is gone, and it is up to all of us to nourish the hope they gave us." Teddy nourished that hope every day in his work in Watts.

Dalili Davis remembers that her husband, who was about four years younger than Ted, had idolized him when they were growing up, but she didn't actually meet Lena's son until she and her husband were in New York and Ted and his family moved there for a while. She recalled:

> He stayed in a house on 139th Street and came around to visit when we were on 140th Street. He wrote poetry and he was highly creative and very philosophical and artistic. He knew he was very ill, and he would come over to just talk while we were scraping wallpaper off the walls and trying to clean up the apartment we were in. He would philosophize on life, and he decided to go on a regimen of herbs and vitamins and minerals at that time.
>
> This short period of time—late 1960s—we became friends with him and his old lady. She was pregnant, and he was very sick. She went to the hospital to have the baby, and he was sick in the hospital at the time the baby was born. We had to contact Lena, and she came immediately, and it was then that I realized the love she had for her son. They didn't see each other much, but you could see that there was a bond.

Lena persuaded Ted to move his family back to Los Angeles,

where Lena was spending most of her time caring for her father, and where she could help him more. As ill as he was, the burden of a new baby was more than he ought to handle alone. "He did come out here," Davis recalls, "and ended up living in the house that had been his father's. His kidney was gone, and he really needed a transplant, but he wouldn't do it. So, she talked him into having a dialysis machine, which cost a lot of money. He would hook himself up on that machine every night, stay on it all night long, get up in the morning and go to work, and come back and hook himself up on it again.

"After about a year, he finally said he didn't see any point to it, that there was no reason for anyone to live under those circumstances; he thought it was degrading and he wanted to just stop. She begged him to stay on it, and they fought about it, but he eventually decided to just give up, and he died very shortly afterwards."

Teddy died September 12, 1970, only about five months after his grandfather. He was twenty-nine years old and left two sons and two daughters. "I hated the world," Lena recalls, "because a mother can't bear to bury a child." But she had known for a long time that he would die.

Completely unexpected, however, was Lennie's death of a heart attack, just a few months later on April 24, 1971. Lena did not immediately react. She couldn't react to any more pain or to the loss of the third important man in her life. In fact, less than a month after his death, she kept an engagement with comedian Alan King at the Westbury Music Fair in New York. It took her six months before the full reality of Lennie's death hit her, and then she simply went numb. "I suddenly ground to a halt. I couldn't do anything. I didn't want to get up in the morning."

Lennie had been her crutch, her anchor, for twenty-four years. Theirs had not been an easy marriage: "I remembered how ashamed we were to be annoyed with each other, to fight with each other, to have the natural hang-ups that married people have. Because, you see, we had to live that careful, exemplary thing. We didn't dare let our marriage fail." But it had been an exceptionally durable marriage, and Lennie had been an exceptional man, shielding Lena from a hostile world when she needed it, letting her stand on her own when she felt she needed to be on her own. He had given her the tools—her professional craft—to enable her to be independent. He had been the one man in her life who was always there for her. Now he, too, was gone and Lena felt as if the tissue of her being had been torn apart.

It took her another four months or so to come out of her somnolent state. As she told John Gruen, "Despite the numbness, I suddenly felt very strong—I felt tremendously alive. I hated it, feeling so strong and alive. All these men left me a kind of tremendous strength to go ahead, to finish the job. I didn't know what the job was, but I ceased to devour myself."

12

REBIRTH

ONE man who was still with Lena was Ralph Harris, her long-time road manager, and he urged her to continue performing. Realizing that he was right, and needing to keep busy, Lena did go back on the road, playing a few club dates. In early March 1972 she again teamed up with Alan King to play the Deauville Star Theatre in Miami Beach. In December she was in Windsor, Ontario, at the Elmwood Theatre, where she told a reporter, "I take less money but at least I am the attraction, hopefully, and not the crap tables." In the spring of 1973 she recorded with Gabor Szabo. She did a few television commercials. She and Harry Belafonte talked about doing a Broadway variety show, a two-or-three-week run, perhaps at the Palace; but they realized the expenses would be prohibitive. "I'm not owned by a big record company so that money wouldn't be coming to us," Lena explained to R. Couri Hay of *Interview* in early 1973. "Our musicians, lights, costumes, people, the rental of the theater would be enormous, unless you charged a certain amount for tickets." She pursued her career in an almost desultory manner.

She much preferred being with Gail and her granddaughters. Having lost Teddy, she figuratively clung to her daughter for a time. She walked the few blocks to Gail's brownstone often and liked to get up at 7 A.M. to watch cartoons with Amy and with Jenny, who had been born two years after Amy. She shopped, she read, she cooked, she listened to music. But she felt a loneliness that she knew only working might assuage, and doing a few club dates and some Skippy Peanut Butter and Tang commercials wasn't enough. What she needed was a focus to her career, and thus, when it was suggested that she do a tour with white singer Tony Bennett, the idea felt right, even though she wondered why Bennett would be interested in "an old black broad like me." And so the two singing stars, who had started out in the 1940s and never before toured with another major star, went out on tour together.

They began the tour in Europe and kicked it off with a British-produced television special called simply "Tony and Lena," which aired in the United States in September 1973. The special showed how successful a combination they were, complementing each other in their singing as well as in their personalities. John J. O'Connor of *The New York Times* called the show "consistently pleasant, frequently superb." Returning from Europe, they took their tandem tour across the North American continent, playing major cities in the United States and Canada.

There was one major city where they didn't appear for their scheduled engagement. Boston, where they were to appear October 23-26, 1974, at Symphony Hall, was so embroiled in racial unrest over busing that, two weeks before their appearance, Lena told Bennett that she couldn't perform in the city. Bennett appreciated her feelings and agreed to the cancellation. Lena made the formal announcement, explaining, "stoning of black children and the beating of black citizens forces me to cancel my appearance," but according to Frances Williams, Lena's friend and a little-theater manager in Los Angeles, "both she and Tony paid all the expenses of the man who had promoted them—all the advance publicity costs, ticket costs, and auditorium costs."

Lena took advantage of the unscheduled vacation to return to New York to visit her mother, who was ill and had been in the hospital for some time. "That's actually, I guess, the reason I'm working again," she told *Women's Wear Daily*—my mother's in the hospital and I've got some whopping bills to pay." Edna Rodriguez allowed Lena to fuss over her when she was ill, and that gave Lena a small sense of the closeness she had been trying to establish with her mother for years.

On October 30, Lena and Tony opened in New York at the Minskoff Theatre on Broadway for two-and-a-half weeks, and the press turned out in droves to see the show, which by this time was technically smooth-running and thoroughly polished. First, Lena and Tony appeared onstage together and sang a medley of "Something," "Look of Love," and "My Funny Valentine." Then Lena sang, alone, a variety of songs—old "Surrey with the Fringe On Top," "Honeysuckle Rose," "A Fine Romance"—and new—"Loneliness," a Stevie Wonder song, even "Being Green" from "Sesame Street" (not for nothing did she watch all that television with her granddaughters). As an encore, of course, "Stormy Weather." Despite the presence of a thirty-two piece orchestra, she relied in many of the numbers on the kind of backup that she had become accustomed to over the years: piano, drums, and guitar played by Gabor Szabo. After an intermission, it was Bennett's turn to sing old standards like "I Left My Heart in San Francisco" and "Just in Time," as well as new songs— "Maybe This Time," "My Love," and "What the World Needs Now." For the finale, Tony and Lena again came together for a dazzling medley of Harold Arlen tunes.

In their reviews of the show, New York critics preferred Bennett not only for his voice but also for his enjoyment in performing. Nat Hentoff wrote in the *Village Voice* that Lena the personality was up on the stage while the real Lena was "somewhere else, away from audiences and from the large orchestra that the stage Lena Horne needs to keep pushing her singing, to help her voice impersonate buoyancy and passion."

A writer for the *New Yorker* didn't see what all the fuss was about: "Lena Horne has been belabored in the local press for her shortcomings as a singer, but her singing has never been more than a prop, a bit of stage business. She is one of nature's nearly flawless constructions, and her work is not to sing but to be observed by as many people as possible. . . . So the ears rest during Lena's half of the evening and the eyes rest during Tony's. Nobody goes to *see* Bennett. . . ."

In New York, Michel Legrand considered Lena sufficiently hearable to ask her to record with him, but she didn't see the event as any sort of justification of her singing. While it's unlikely that she read any of the New York reviews of her half of the show with Bennett, she'd long ago decided that she would never be a great singer. Her voice had never been strong, and she had not come out of the same background as the great soul singers she admired. Aretha Franklin, after all, had the church—the traditional black, Baptist church—for centuries the only place where blacks had total freedom of expression. Lena had been baptized a Catholic, and although she had joined the Baptist church for her first husband, the Pittsburgh middle-class Baptists to whom she was exposed were a far cry from the Southern Baptist tradition. Somewhere she had read Roberta Flack's comment that Lena might not sound black but [in her opinion she] had a tremendous amount of soul, and that pleased Lena.

Equally pleasing was the respect she received from other, younger singers whom she admired—Dionne Warwick, Lola Falana, Mary Wilson. Back in 1972, in San Francisco, she had appeared with Billy Eckstine at the Circle Star Theater and had been visited backstage by these women, who had formed Bravo, an unofficial association of female singers. They presented her with a ring and thanked her for having been a trailblazer who had made it easier for them to pursue their careers. Lena was gratified that they appreciated her, even though, in the typical fashion of youth, they said that they wanted her to know how they felt "while you're still alive." She was fifty-five at the time.

While she still felt very much alive, Lena was beginning to shed some of the emotional trappings of youth. She was starting to feel as if possessions were relatively unimportant and was grateful for that feeling when, the week before Christmas 1974, she was robbed of all the jewelry her father had left her. She had sold the house in Palm Springs and never intended to own a house again; the small, two-room apartment near Gail suited her needs just fine.

From New York, Tony and Lena wended their way across the country, arriving on the West Coast in March, where they were a smash hit at the Shubert in Los Angeles and where the critics were considerably kinder to Lena than the New York critics had been. For Lena it was a nice way to end what had been a very satisfying period in her professional life, and despite what critics like Hentoff said, she began to feel herself opening up to her audiences in a way that she hadn't been able to do before.

Returning to New York, Lena looked around for something different to do. There had been plans for her to do a syndicated talk show called "Lena's Grapevine," with Hugh Downs as producer, and she would have loved that, but it hadn't materialized. She was approached by Gene Kelly to costar with Ben Vereen in an adaptation of the Rodgers and Hart classic, *Pal Joey*, and she was very enthusiastic about the idea; but the stage show was in the planning stages only, and she knew it would be a while before it would occupy her time. So she went back on the road. She toured with Vic Damone and with the Count Basie Orchestra, played the Fairmont Hotels in San Francisco, New Orleans, and Dallas, even did another European tour. But Europe had not been the same for her since Lennie's death; without Lennie to turn to it was not as exciting to see some new part of the continent. In New York, between tours, she visited her mother, but that relationship was still not satisfying, and she spent so much time with Gail and her family that she began to feel like a clinging grandmother. "I was getting overprotective," she explains. She was thinking that she needed to put some more space between herself and her family when she was robbed a second time, and that persuaded her to leave New York. It wasn't the same city that she had fallen in love with so many decades before; she found the bag ladies and the dirty streets depressing. And so, although she had vowed never again to own a house, she bought one on the West Coast.

She chose Santa Barbara because it was "a beautiful compromise between San Francisco and New York. San Francisco is best but it's too far from my work." She wanted to be close enough to the ABC and NBC studios to do television, if the opportunity arose. She bought the house "just because I fell in love with it," she told a reporter. "I must be crazy. Thirty years older than God and buying a house for no other reason than that I fell in love with it." The house, on a one-acre plot, was a converted olive mill, two-storied, stone on the ground floor, clapboard on the second; inside, the walls were rough stone and wood paneled, and Lena looked forward to decorating it and planting flowers and trees outside. She planted the flowers, and a few trees, first. Inside, she had installed an elaborate stereo system that allowed music to be piped throughout the house, and she provided most of the rooms with basic furnishings. She also had an elaborate security system put in. But she found that she was not inspired to do much decorating; she also realized that she was lonely.

In 1977, Dalili Davis was in the process of divorcing her husband and wondering what to do without a job or money, when her mother-in-law, Elois, called her to ask: "How would you like to work for Lena for a while? She can't pay you much—just wants some company—but she can give you something." Davis accepted the offer immediately and arrived in Santa Barbara expecting to stay for approximately two months. Davis recalls:

"We went shopping and picked out materials. They were all her ideas. She had different rooms that she wanted to decorate in different flavors. One room that I loved very much was upstairs. It was supposed to be sort of a guest room, but it was really her little writing room and she had all white wicker furniture and lots of little bright pastel pillows. And pictures—pictures of her family *everywhere*—all over this room. I imagine that it was her spirit room, where when she got lonely or when she missed somebody she could go to just sort of get the vibrations from the ancestors.

182

"The other thing that knocked me out was her attic. It was loaded with records and books—plus wardrobe, but it was the records and books that impressed me. She had Louis Armstrong records from way back when he was a teenager in New Orleans. She had a wealth of Aretha and Carmen McCrae, and when I got ahold of those albums, and that speaker system . . . ! One day Carmen called up and Lena said, 'Carmen, I got Elois's daughter-in-law over here, and all I hear is your mouth! That girl loves you to death!'

"One evening we were just sitting and talking and I was asking her about different performers. She said that she worshipped Aretha, the freedom she expressed. She said she always wanted to be that free but she had to always be proper. 'Aretha,' she said, 'does what she wants to do, and just listen to her music. Why, I could be her toe jam.' Lena really does use that kind of language.

"And all those books. When you look at her library, you know why she is so aware—the life of Frederick Douglass, of W.E.B. DuBois. She'd read all those books. She loves to read—that's what she does in her *prime* time, and then she looks at late movies. I asked why, and she said, 'You know, the world is so messed up. I like to go back and see when things were pret-ty. Where there was humor. It just relaxes me to go back into those times.'

"She was so down-to-earth. She liked the yard best, and growing vegetables and flowers. She loved to get out there in the dirt, work with her hands. She was friends with her housekeeper, a young girl who was going to college. My mother-in-law's sister-in-law lived in Santa Barbara, and because of that family connection Lena would call them when she wanted Louisiana hot link sausage. Or they'd call her to come over and get some fresh-caught fish. She loved that. She loved to be in family situations, around people who didn't make a fuss about her. They just worship her, but they know not to make a fuss because it makes her uncomfortable.

"She really doesn't like to be treated like anyone special. When a girl friend of mine heard I was going to stay with Lena she begged me to get an autographed picture. I knew I shouldn't ask—Lena told me right at first that she likes her privacy—but I'd told my girlfriend I'd try. That was a mistake. Lena got very cold, very frank: 'Oh, please—I cannot understand this. It doesn't make any sense—people are human beings. No, I just *don't* like to do it.' She believed in the equality of human beings, and it was a principle that she wanted to maintain.

"That was the only time I saw her go cold, although when we were talking she said she was bitter about some people, talked about back-stabbing and all that. I noticed one time when we went out that she put makeup on, and I said, 'You know, you don't need that makeup.' She said, 'Listen. These people think I got face-lifts. Everywhere I go, somebody wants to lift up my eyelid, look up underneath, to see if I've got real eyeballs. When I go out, I just like to make sure that I look good. These people write articles—they just want to find something so they can say, oh, she's deteriorating!'

"We did a lot of talking. She has a little couch and a TV in the kitchen. She loves to cook and didn't want me to do any of the cooking. She'll do red snapper and things like that, but she likes to get down into some greens and some blackeye peas and corn bread. I'd be sitting on the couch, feeling nervous because I wasn't doing anything to help, and she'd say, 'Just relax, I'm just glad to have the company.' After we'd eaten we'd sit on the couch and watch TV and talk. What impressed me most about her was that she was just *discovering herself*—at that age, at that date. It was really inspiring, and I know that's what she wanted me to feel. I was so down in the dumps, coming out of a fifteen-year marriage without enough skills, feeling very bitter. She was building up my confidence, making me think positively. I could tell just by the intensity of the way she dealt with me that she was trying to save me from going through what, evidently, she had gone through—a period of low self-esteem. She was like an excited baby—excited about her music, excited about her touring, excited about decorating her house.

"Then, when I had been there just a few days, she got a phone call from New York—her daughter or someone saying that her mother had died. She just sat down for a while, and I could tell there was a lot of feeling there, but she didn't let it out at that time. She got her things together, got packed just like a business woman, had me take her to the airport in the little Volvo she'd bought for me to drive her around in. She said, 'Do anything you want. Forget about working. Just water the garden, don't let my flowers die. Make sure everything is locked and keep the alarm system on.' By the time she got back, the time I was supposed to spend with her was over, and then she had to go on tour. So she wasn't able to do what she wanted with the house.''

Back in New York, Lena buried her mother without ever having made the kind of peace with her that she would have liked. "I understood my mother," she told Marcia Gillespie of *Ms.* Magazine in the summer of 1981, "but she didn't want to understand me. She in some ways was younger than I, in that she just wouldn't compromise: she was thwarted in what she wanted and nothing compensated. She didn't approve of the way I handled my career. She said she would have done it better, been bigger longer. She believed that had she had the chance she would have done more with it."

When her mother died, Lena was not relieved that the battle she and her mother had waged for nearly half a century, ever since she had quit show business to marry Louis, was over. In fact she realized that, in an odd fashion, it has been their way of communicating and that a small part of her had continued to want to please her mother. Now, with her mother gone, she felt she really had no one left to please. It took her a while to realize that she still had to please herself.

After her mother's funeral, Lena spent some time in New York with Gail and her family. At the time, Sidney Lumet was hard at work on a black movie musical version of *The Wizard of Oz*, which had already been a hit on Broadway as *The Wiz*, starring Stephanie Mills as Dorothy. The movie version, to be produced by Motown, would star Diana Ross as Dorothy and Richard Pryor as the title character. Lena was excited about the project and unabashedly pressured her son-in-law to include her. Lumet agreed to cast her as the good witch, Glinda. "I wanted to play the bad witch so badly," she told an interviewer for *Applause* in April 1978, "but my son-in-law said, 'You're stuck with your image, Lena, suffer!'" So, when rehearsals started in August 1977, Lena polished up her goody-two-shoes persona and put her heart into the song, "If You Believe." The movie, which premiered in New York in October 1978, was the most expensive all-black film ever produced; it was also a critical disaster and a box-office failure.

Unfortunately, by the time the movie premiered, Gail and Sidney Lumet were in the process of divorce. During the months of filming, the marriage had hit the rocks, but both Lena and her son-in-law managed to put their professionalism above their personal feelings. Lena made a point of not getting involved, except to advise her daughter, "Rise above it, baby. Go on and cry and bitch and carry on. We are strong ladies." As soon as her work on *The Wiz* was over, she returned to Santa Barbara. But privately she agonized over the divorce. "It really hurt me," she told Marie Brenner of *New York,* "and it took me a few years to realize that Gail had never been on her own. She had always been Lena Horne's daughter or Sidney Lumet's wife."

From Santa Barbara she commuted to Los Angeles where, at last, the adaptation of *Pal Joey* was finally to be realized. The show had suffered a very difficult birth. Originally Lena was to have costarred with Ben Vereen. "But we didn't know 'Roots' was going to happen and put Ben so far out in space," Lena explained. The idea was put on the shelf. A little while later she was approached with the idea of a television miniversion of the show in which she would play opposite Sammy Davis, Jr. Again she said yes, and again the idea died, this time over problems with the rights. Finally, in early 1978, the idea was resurrected, this time as a vehicle for Tony-nominee Clifton Davis. Lena said yes a third time to the offer of the role of Vera, the older, well-to-do woman who is infatuated with the young, ne'er-do-well Joey, and this time the show actually went into rehearsals.

To keep up with the young chorus girls and boys, Lena took dance instruction every morning and followed a Spartan regimen that she described simply as "suffering." But she enjoyed it immensely, especially working with the young people to whom, in many ways, she felt closer than she did to her peers. Interviewed in a dance studio at the Music Center in Los Angeles by Judith Friedel of *Applause*, she was asked if the cast were all black. Lena responded that one of the wonderful things about the show was that black and white people were working together. Friedel said she hadn't seen any white faces passing by, and Lena responded, "Well, they all look alike, don't they? They talk alike when they're young, wear each other's clothes, use each other's hairdos. . . ." She pointed to Friedel's permed hair, and they both laughed.

The character of Vera had been altered from that of a rich, bored, spoiled woman to a working woman who'd come up the hard way, and Lena liked that. She also liked the way musical director John Myles arranged the classic songs from the original show to sound contemporary, among them "Bewitched," which Vera sang about her feelings for Joey. There was a sense of camaraderie among the cast, and for Lena, working on *Pal Joey* was like old home week. Claude Thompson, who had been in the chorus of *Jamaica*, was the choreographer, and Josephine Premice, who had also been in the *Jamaica* cast, played the character of Melba in *Pal Joey*. The conductor was John Myles, who had been musical director on the television show, "Monsanto Night Presents Lena Horne," and Frances Williams, den mother to black Hollywood for years, and a long-time friend, was an adviser. Williams recalls that Lena was relaxed and spontaneous. At one point a friend of Williams's who owned a restaurant sent over a dozen sweet-potato pies for the cast and crew. "Lena said, 'I ain't sharin' this with nobody. I'm takin' *mine* home!'"

Everyone involved had great hopes for the success of the show, which premiered in San Diego April 4-15, was scheduled to go on to Los Angeles and San Francisco, and from there, hopefully, to New York. Unfortunately, it was not sufficiently well received on the West Coast, closing after twenty-six weeks, and never made it to New York. At age sixty Lena was left in superb shape but bereft of the opportunity to dance.

"It's funny," Lena told Friedel, "but when I was young I thought forty was the end of everything. People would constantly remind me of my age. Even when I was thirty, people would say with amazement, 'Why, Lena, you're still looking so good.' You have to remember that when I started out, my business was very rough on a woman." Looking back, she realized that it hadn't been until her forties that she had lost her Victorian hang-ups about sex, and not until her fifties that she had really begun to enjoy performing. Thus, when she turned sixty she wondered what new stage of growth was in store for her.

She suspected that whatever it was, it would affect her professional life more than her private life. Although she could get lonely sometimes, she was relatively happy being alone. When Gail and Sidney had divorced, Gail had moved to an apartment in the Lincoln Center area on Manhattan's West Side, and Lena had taken an apartment nearby. She enjoyed visiting New York, although she didn't want to live there permanently anymore, and she liked spending time with her daughter and granddaughters. She also visited Teddy's children in Los Angeles as often as she could, but she enjoyed the house in Santa Barbara and working in her garden. She'd planted some fifty fruit trees on the property and wanted to nourish them into healthy growth. She didn't want to marry again, not only because there were few eligible men her age (and she had no intention of taking up with a younger man), but also because she wasn't sure she had the energy to make another marriage work. She still felt sexy, but, as she told an interviewer for *Ebony* in 1980, "I'm stuck with a kind of romantic attitude about sex. I only like to go to bed with people I really like. As a result, I keep to myself a lot. That way, I don't get too itchy about finding a man." No, she had her books and her records and the few friends from the old days who were still alive—by 1980, both her Uncle Frank and her Uncle Burke had died—and she didn't expect her personal life to change very much.

Over the years her professional life had changed and much of it hadn't been her doing. Many of the changes she'd gone through were a result of the changing times, and as she faced returning to the stage in the late 1970s she also faced the fact that the number of stages on which she preferred to perform had shrunk drastically. She liked glamorous hotel entertainment rooms. In these, the audiences sat and listened and weren't distracted by gambling tables, as they were in Las Vegas, or clinking glasses and romantic assignations, as they were in the small cabarets. They were big enough so that an entertainer could command the audience's attention, but not so big that the entertainer felt swallowed up. But these rooms were becoming fewer and fewer. The Empire Room at the Waldorf-Astoria was gone; the Copacabana brought in big-name stars only occasionally; even the Riviera, across the Hudson in New Jersey, was gone, and Lena could remember when it had first opened and its first owner had secured her promise to work there by assuring her that its admissions policy would be strictly nondiscriminatory. The same was true in other cities; people just didn't dress up and go out to such places anymore. The big places that remained were so huge, like Madison Square Garden, Radio City Music Hall, and the Hollywood Bowl, that an entertainer like Lena just felt insignificant on their stages. Cabarets had made a comeback—they proliferated in New York—but Lena had said good-bye to the "rooms" long ago. There were few in-between places left, and so, when Lena played the Westbury Music Fair on Long Island in March 1979, it was the first time she had appeared in the New York area in five years.

Appearing on a bill with composer Marvin Hamlisch, Lena gave New York-area audiences a sense of the changes that had occurred in her as a professional. John S. Wilson of *The New York Times* identified "an intensity, sometimes warm and intimate, sometimes ominously commanding, in every syllable that she projects." He noted, too, Lena's new, more relaxed stage presence. For the first time, she was allowing her audience to know her and not worrying about her image. She joked about sweating onstage: "I'm the world's greatest sweater." A decade earlier, on the set of *Patch/Death of a Gunfighter*, she had confided to an interviewer that she didn't want to appear sweaty. She engaged in light patter between numbers, something she'd never done in stage appearances before, although she had tried it once on a British-produced TV special. She seemed truly to enjoy her audiences, and Dalili Davis recalls that during the time she was staying with Lena in Santa Barbara, Lena had expressed excitement about onstage performing: "First of all, you have to feel the applause, to know that when you get up there, even though you're afraid to do it, it's worth it. Once you've tasted that appreciation and that love coming from the audience, then, all the butterflies— which *I still get*—are just secondary to what you know you're going to receive."

But places like the Westbury Music Fair were getting scarce, and for all her energy and her new-found enjoyment of audiences, Lena did feel as if, at sixty-plus, she ought to retire. After all, she was beginning to see herself in the "old movies" on television and was being called "a living legend" to her face. Still, she kept getting invitations to perform and kept enjoying the experience. In May 1980 she did a benefit at the Kennedy Center for the Duke Ellington School of Arts and received no fewer than four standing ovations from the audience, who had paid anywhere from $100 to $240 to see her. After the show, Lena said, "I always say I'm going to stop performing, but then I get an audience like the one tonight and I get all corny again."

Sherman Sneed, who had taken over from Ralph Harris as her road agent (Harris remained with her) didn't like to have the situation so up in the air. He feared Lena might do some relatively unheralded benefit somewhere and then, for no particular reason, never perform in concert again. "Do you want to go out with a bang or with a whimper?" he asked her. Of course, she preferred the bang. They talked about a one-woman show as early as 1979, but nothing came of it. So Sneed pursued the next best idea: a "farewell" concert tour. Once Lena had agreed there was no problem getting the backing. Delta Sigma Theta, with which Lena had continued to work over the years, agreed to sponsor a two-month series of benefits.

Lena's farewell tour began in mid-June 1980, with a benefit for the Joan Robinson Fuselier Memorial Fund at the Ahmanson

Theater in Los Angeles. It ended in August. Everywhere she appeared critics praised the warmth of her balladry, her "looseness" on the stage. Lena, who didn't read critical reviews, went off to sing at the Sporting Club gala in Monte Carlo, an institution where *she* had become an institution. On her return, she'd told herself, she would devote her time to gardening in Santa Barbara. She had done her farewell tour, and she wasn't going to be like Muhammad Ali and come back out of retirement.

13

LIVING
LEGEND

SHERMAN Sneed wasn't satisfied to let Lena retire after a farewell benefit tour, and, upon reflection, neither was Lena. They
both wanted her to go out with a bang, and the only place to do so
was Broadway. Lena wanted to do a musical, but she wanted to do
something new, not a revival, and most of the black shows making it to Broadway were revivals or shows that were based on old
themes. Both she and Sneed contacted various Broadway producers and theater owners in an attempt to unearth some new property that could serve as a vehicle for her. James Nederlander, of the
theater-owning family, said he didn't have any properties for
Lena, but he offered to finance a touring concert show in which
she would be teamed with Sergio Franchi. Lena, however, wasn't
interested in sharing the concert stage with another singer again.
The idea of a one-woman show was actually a compromise: a
project on which both sides were willing to work. Nederlander got
Michael Frazier and Fred Walker to coproduce the show and he
offered as the stage the aging Nederlander Theatre on West 41st
Street. It was booked for a maximum of six weeks, although a

four-week run is generally considered successful for one-person shows.

While taking any show to Broadway involves risks, and while Lena was not exactly a Broadway veteran, the limb on which Nederlander, Frazier, and Walker went out was not as weak as it might have been a couple of years earlier: the 1981 season seemed to be shaping up as a veritable celebration of Broadway's past and of the durable female performers who had lighted up both screen and stage in years gone by—the names of Elizabeth Taylor, Lauren Bacall, and Katherine Hepburn would all be on Broadway theater marquees. In Lena's opinion, if they could do it, so could she.

But once the necessary agreements had been signed she had some second thoughts. She knew that she hadn't been very well received when she appeared with Tony Bennett at the Minskoff Theatre six years before. She realized that her experience on Broadway had been limited; she wondered if she'd be able to carry off a two-hour show all by herself. She went through her usual period of soul-searching before she determined that "there was only one place to finish and the place was Broadway." As she explained to Michiko Kakutani of *The New York Times* a week before the show opened, "I never thought I'd be working at my age, but you get caught up in the gratification of feeling you're a worker . . . you get into the habit of surviving."

Lena, Sneed, who would be billed as an associate producer, and Ralph Harris went to work immediately. They decided that the show ought to have a book, and Samm-Art Williams, the black playwright whose *Home* had first been presented off-Broadway by the Negro Ensemble Company and done so well that it had been taken to Broadway, was employed to write it. The next question was, what should Lena sing? Over the years she had sung hundreds of songs; a few had become so closely associated with her that she had to include them, but there were other, new songs, that she wanted to sing. In fact, she wanted to sing some songs that were brand-new. Friends submitted lists of songs they thought she ought to include. Others submitted lists of songs they thought she ought not to include, because the material wasn't right for Broadway. After a few weeks, Lena wasn't so sure she wanted to go through with the show after all.

Samm-Art Williams was working in a heavy vein, relating Lena's life to the black American experience. It seemed too serious to Lena. It seemed to reflect her feelings in the 1960s rather than the way she felt in 1980. Certainly, she felt angry sometimes about the plight of her people, and there was a lot about society that she thought should change, but she had lost her interest in crusading. Reading about her life as presented by Williams, and as she herself had once viewed it, she got depressed. She didn't want to relive it that way. "Some young chick who wants to go through it all can do it," she decided.

Lena had already interspersed biographical bits with songs in her performances, the first time being in her British-produced special back in the late 1960s. American critics hadn't thought much of her banter on TV, but she found that live audiences liked it. More important, she'd found that *she* liked it. "The first time I talked I was fifty," she told John Corry of *The New York Times*. "I don't know—I can make people laugh. When I hear the audience laugh, I think, Oh, my God! I'm funny!" That's how she wanted to be in her one-woman show—funny—and so Samm-Art Williams's association with the project ended and Lena, with considerable help from her co-workers, began to write her own "book."

It was written casually, after the basic chronological sequence had been established. Lena and Luther Henderson, the show's musical consultant, worked out the Cotton Club sequence during an engagement in Toronto. Luther Henderson and Lena went way back—and even if he hadn't been at the Cotton Club himself, Henderson remembered the tunes of the era. Other sequences were written with the help of Sherman Sneed, whom Lena credits with knowing what ought to be included and what ought not and what would give the audience the most enjoyment, which was what Lena wanted. She wanted to have fun, and she wanted the audience to have fun. Simple as that.

Cutting down the number of songs was not so simple. Lena had wanted to do some new material, and she insisted on doing a song by Charlie Smalls, who had written the music for *The Wiz*, called "That's What Miracles Are All About" and one by Martin Charnin, who'd written the music for *Annie*, called "Fly." To make room for them she was quite willing to give up a couple of her traditional and, she believed, rather tired songs, among them her trademark. Lena didn't want to sing "Stormy Weather"; she was tired of singing "Stormy Weather." Sneed and others insisted that she must. When she went into rehearsals, alone, at the Broadway Arts Rehearsal Hall on February 16, 1981, the question of "Stormy Weather" was still up in the air, and over the next two-and-a-half months it was taken out and put back in so often that it became a running joke. Eventually, it was decided that Lena sing it not once, but twice, as a way of showing her growth as a singer. The first time, she would sing it dispassionately, almost in a rote manner, to emphasize the paucity of emotion in her earlier singing. But the second time she would sing it in a way that would make the song seem almost new, as if she'd never sung it before. That, Lena knew, would surely convince her audience that she was a skilled actress.

To make the first half of the show a reminiscence of Lena's past and the second half a statement of Lena in the present, they had to work hard at paring down her repertoire. In the end, they had to discard the idea of equal amounts of new and traditional music because the show was running too long—three hours by the time the choreographer began to stage the numbers for Lena and the three members of her company. Some contemporary songs like the Beatles's "You Can't Win" and "Don't It Make You Want to Go Home" were cut, and the majority of songs that were retained were composed before 1950. But each one had a special meaning to Lena and a specific reference to her life.

Meanwhile, the conducting staff underwent a change. Lena had insisted on hiring the musicians and conductor personally and she had hired Linda Twine as an assistant conductor. Twine, a thirty-six-year-old former classical pianist, had been assistant conductor for *The Wiz* on Broadway, and she impressed **Lena** when she brought a tape recorder to rehearsals so she could study Lena's interpretation of the music. Thus, when the show's conductor left just before the previews, Lena suspected that Twine could step in and take over without seriously affecting the show; in fact, she suspected that Twine might enhance the show, not only because of her conducting talents but because she was that rare item: a black, woman conductor on Broadway. Broadway orchestras are quite rigidly segregated. Except for black shows the faces in the pit are almost exclusively white, and even for black shows the conductor is usually white. By having a black female conductor for her show, Lena made another breakthrough, although it was quite unintentional. She simply took the person who was best for the job.

As the opening date for the show drew closer, still another problem arose. Lena wasn't satisfied to have just three backup singers/dancers for the Cotton Club scene in Act I. Back at the real Cotton Club in 1933, there had been five, and that's how Lena wanted it. The director, Arthur Faria, said no—the $325,000 budget was tight as it was and didn't allow for the addition of extra personnel at such a late date. Lena continued to insist, and the star and her director were barely on speaking terms when the show went into previews.

Lena Horne: The Lady and Her Music went into previews on April 30, 1981. The show was still running too long, two hours and forty minutes, but the audiences didn't seem to mind. They bought $41,500 worth of tickets. In the second week of previews, Lena and company had managed to pare about fifteen minutes from the show, and $92,400 worth of tickets were sold. By opening night, the show was down to the length that it would remain, two hours and ten minutes, and the next day alone people bought $70,000 worth of tickets. Within two days after its opening on May 12, 1981, the announcement was made that the show's limited engagement would be extended.

The show was "a triumph!" and since the show was Lena and Lena was the show, she was a triumph. For at least a decade, even critics who could find nothing particularly notable about her voice had mentioned her "presence" onstage; but now she *commanded* the stage. And she commanded her material. In its final, honed-down version, the show contained only songs that either expressed what had happened to her or how she felt, and thus she was able to imbue every single one of them with her personal stamp. But the songs themselves were only part of what made *Lena Horne: The Lady and Her Music* so remarkable an experience. Somehow, the air of excitement was tangible from the moment Linda Twine appeared on stage to strike up the overture. The sight of a black woman conductor was special. And things only got better after that.

Lena swept onto the stage, gorgeous, glamorous, the sight almost everyone in the audience had really come to see. She extended one arm to the audience, palm up, as though inviting them to rise and take a bow: "*How* does she manage to suggest that the drumroll of applause is really for the rest of us and not for her?" wondered Walter Kerr of *The New York Times*. Then she launched into "From This Moment On" with such conviction that the evening from there on would be exciting for both her and the audience that the audience was captivated immediately by her style, her energy. She followed with Jim Croce's "I Got a Name" and let it be known that it was for her father, that she was carrying on his name, and by the time she scream-sang the line "I ain't gonna let life pass me by," those in the audience who were easily moved to tears by the sheer emotion of a moment were misty-eyed. The *second song* was a show-stopper!

But it was only a building block in the production's plan, which had, overall, such an exquisite sense of timing that it was hard to analyze. Carefully paced show-stoppers proliferated. In Broadway parlance, a good show has an "eleven o'clock number" that is climactic, that brings the audience to such an emotional height that it goes limp. Lena's show had these numbers without end. It was something Lennie had taught her: to imbue each song with dramatic thrust. Each of the songs was not only sung by Lena, it *was* Lena: "Yesterday, When I Was Young," "Life Goes

On," "If You Believe," "That's What Miracles Are All About." They said, in effect, "Yeah, I'm getting on, but life doesn't end with the end of youth; believe in yourself and watch what happens." It was a message that the audience wanted to get, whether its members were balding white men who had secretly adored Lena for years (and there were a lot of them), or women who also were getting on and who could take heart in her energy and fight, or youngsters who'd always thought life ended at thirty.

Not just in her songs but also in her "dialogues," Lena affirmed more than her own life. She affirmed life itself—"good old sweet, hard life," as she said in one of her personal lyrics to "I Got a Name." She reviewed the hard times of her career with a retrospective humor, and in like manner she touched upon her own personal changes. Middle-class members of the audience—and at the price of Broadway tickets there weren't too many poor folks in the seats—might have been a bit put off at first by her "git-down" persona. After all, her image for forty-odd years had been ice-cold and proper, and so this warm, quintessentially earthy Lena was something of a surprise. But in the course of her dialogues Lena somehow conveyed that at the age of fifty she had decided to behave exactly as she felt, which meant getting "trashy"—"traa-sheh," as she put it—whenever she felt like it. She personified a mesmerizing contradiction. As Walter Kerr wrote, "Because she is so elegantly high-style, she is free to be low—deliciously low as she does a field hand shuffle beneath that Greek gown. Because she is so articulate, she is free to adopt whatever language amuses her, tossing off 'git' for 'got' in the middle of an effably precise sentence. . . . She looks as though she could be easily shattered, as easily as spun glass; that enables her to be tough."

Lena strode around that stage as if she owned it. She paced it like a tiger. At times, it seemed too small to encompass her presence. But always she conveyed an intimacy with her audience that was impossible to analyze. She had them even when she turned her back on them for an entire number. On leaving the theater one young woman announced to no one in particular, "I feel as if *I* have just entertained *her*." Whatever their feelings, audiences left the Nederlander Theater knowing that they had just been treated to a bona fide *experience.*

New York audiences are not easily awestruck; and if New York audiences are hard nuts to crack, New York critics are like fossil nuts. They are a singularly unsentimental lot, otherwise, they wouldn't have been so hard on Lena's singing back in 1974 during her first major tour after the deaths of her father, son, and husband. It takes something extraordinary to stimulate them to write words like *triumph* and *incomparable* and *awesome,* but in their reviews of Lena's one-woman show they were sprinkling these words around like salt. It was as if they were seeing her for the first time. Wrote Walter Kerr:

> We all recognize Miss Horne, of course. From a few films, per-haps; possibly from her only other Broadway musical show appearance in *Jamaica*; from an evening at the Waldorf. And of course she must have devotees who've followed her here, there and everywhere—gradually adding up her astonishing effects one by two, four by 10. But all at once, sustained for more than two hours, gentling and/or exploding 25 or more songs in a row? With virtually no help? Certainly I'd never been exposed to this experience. And that means I didn't *know* the performer at all.

A lot of other people decided it was time to meet the new Lena; her audience read like a *Who's Who* practically every night. New York's paparazzi found that they need only station themselves outside the Nederlander Theater—the stars would come to them. First Lady Nancy Reagan was just about the only luminary who didn't have trouble getting tickets. During the intermission she went to Lena's dressing room and the two laughed together about their days under contract with MGM, although Lena's days had preceded Nancy's. MGM reared its head again in the person of David Begelman, before his fall. He sent flowers with a note that read, "Dear Lena, Please come back to Hollywood, give us another chance. Maybe this time we'll do better by you." There was no peace for Lena during the twenty-minute intermission in each show—the stars wanted to go backstage to see her. Liza Minnelli, Paul Newman and Joanne Woodward, Coretta Scott King, Jacqueline Onassis, the list was endless. Each received the same warm greeting; Lena was past resenting the fact that not all these people had been her friends before. If they wanted to be her friends now, she was pleased to welcome them.

She was pleased, too, to accept the special Tony that was awarded her on June 7, although she commented "Well, it's about time." One-person shows are not eligible for regular Tony awards, but there was no question that the Tony Awards committee had to do something to recognize the woman whose show was putting into shadow everything else on Broadway. The committee would have voted to give her the special award anyway, but a social worker in Brooklyn had decided not to leave the matter to chance. George Andrews had been a fan of Lena's since he had seen her in *Stormy Weather* when he was in ninth grade; he'd seen *Jamaica* eighteen times; he'd collected her records. He was one of those die-hard devotees whom Walter Kerr had suspected were out there somewhere, and he determined that Lena should receive a Tony. On May 16 he had started collecting signatures on a petition to present to the Tony Awards committee, and the twenty thousand signatures he garnered were no doubt mostly those of Brooklynites. Brooklyn hadn't forgotten Lena. Nor had she forgotten her home borough: that summer she sponsored a kids' baseball team in Brooklyn; they decided to call themselves "Lena's Coyotes."

By early June, *Lena Horne: The Lady and Her Music* had been extended indefinitely, and Lena was game to go on for as long as she could. But not with air conditioning—Freon made her sick. The air conditioning was put on before the show, to cool off the theater, but it was turned off well before she appeared. Most members of her audiences didn't even notice; and if they did, they assumed the lack of air conditioning was natural to the old theater. Perhaps old equipment was responsible for the close call

201

of June 19, when a horizontal pole holding twenty lights separated in the middle and swung toward the stage as she began to sing "From This Moment On."

The capacity audience saw the pole falling behind her before she did. They gasped, and some stretched out their arms as if to catch her as the pole fell behind her. Sherman Sneed ran out to her and, throwing his arm around her, led her to her dressing room. "I'll be back," she called over her shoulder to the audience, but she was visibly shaken. When a quick assessment of the damage to the pole indicated that repairs would take at least an hour, it was decided to cancel the performance and offer the audience either a refund or tickets for another show. Lena made the announcement herself. "Please come back," she said, and the inconvenienced audience gave her a standing ovation.

The one aspect of the old Lena Horne that had come through all the changes was her professionalism. As she celebrated her sixty-fourth birthday, she was maintaining a schedule that would prove impossible for other, much younger Broadway stars to take. Whether she was feeling depressed, or ill, or just plain tired, she went on. Certainly, she paced herself—she didn't waste energy on other things because she couldn't—she got to the theater by five o'clock for an eight o'clock performance so she wouldn't have to rush to get ready. Onstage she was so energetic that she lost two or three pounds a show, eight shows a week, including three matinees. And she wasn't eating right. She was grabbing a taco or a hamburger because she didn't feel like concentrating on cooking when she needed all the concentration she could muster for performing. But all that seemed to affect her little. It was as if she got all the nourishment she needed from her audiences, from the image of herself that they projected back at her, from the awe that she knew she inspired. She was glad that she was an incredible example of retarded aging, knew that a substantial portion of her audience every night came primarily to look and then got completely caught up in her voice and her personality and the sharing and the celebration of life that were her primary reasons for being on the stage. "I want them to walk out of that theater *happy*," she said. "And to be saying, 'Jesus, how does that old broad do it?'"

Still, she didn't "do it" completely on her own. "I don't know what I'd do if I didn't have a strong manager and a producer who happens to be black," she told Gil Noble of "Like It Is." "He fights for me. I can fight, but I like somebody tougher to be the heavy. I don't want to fight with management and then get out there and be for my audience. This way, some strong man is taking the flak and fighting back, and all I have to do is walk out there and be open with the audience." Jonathan Schwartz of the *Village Voice* noticed how Sneed treated Lena as Linda Twine struck up the overture and Lena prepared to go on stage: "Sherman Sneed steps in front of her. Gently, he bends over and kisses her right cheek, and kisses her left cheek. He gives his eyes to her. His eyes are saying: I love you, take my strength. He speaks not a word. He slips away. He will watch, as usual, from the back of the auditorium." Sneed provided the anchor that Lena needed. He put up with her depressions and the periods when she was high-strung and overwrought. He was yet another father figure in Lena's life, and she was not ashamed to admit that she needed him. Over the years, and particularly in recent years, she had come to realize that there are a very few people on whom one can and ought to depend.

Given that she was the personification of life experience, a certified veteran of living, there was some irony in Lena's being given the Dance Theatre of Harlem's annual "Emergence Award" in late January 1982, but Lena accepted it graciously. It was only one of a comparative avalanche of awards that poured in on her as her city and her profession honored her. *Lena Horne: The Lady and Her Music* received, in addition to the special Tony award, a Drama Desk Award and a special citation from the New York Drama Critics' Circle. The sound track of the show, produced by Quincy Jones, received two Grammy awards. Lena herself received New York City's highest cultural award, the Handel Medallion, and she was honored by any number of other local organizations. In the space of nine months, she got more awards and more national press coverage than she had received in any nine-year period previously, and she also achieved a notoriety that was unexpected as well as unique. She was probably the first national celebrity to face a "maternity charge."

Page One of the New York *Amsterdam News* of May 22, 1982, carried the headline, "Lena Is My Mom" and the story of Annie Steele, herself a grandmother of four, who claimed that she was Lena Horne's daughter and had been trying to contact her "mother" since she had arrived in New York from Leaf, Alabama, in 1963. She had not seen Lena since she was eight or nine, because Lena had been "on the road," but she said she was convinced that Lena was her mother.

According to Annie Steele, Lena Horne was really Ora Wiley of Alabama. She had become pregnant and had gone home to Alabama to give birth to her daughter, whom she had left there to be brought up by relatives. She would visit occasionally; during the last visit, she argued with her relatives, who threatened to sue her to recover the money they had spent bringing up Annie, and then she left to go and live in Berkeley, California. Who was Annie Steele's father? Steele said, "My great-grandmother, Queen Esther Wiley, who said I was born at home, told me he was Joe Louis."

Steele, who said she believed she was in her forties but had no birth certificate, had written to the Johnson Publishing Company in 1980, after *Ebony* had published an interview with Lena in which she described her relationship with Joe Louis in the early 1940s as close—"he was the only man I was seeing at that time." In the letter, Steele had told her story and sent photographs of herself and the great-uncle in whose home she had been raised and who, she said, was Lena's father's brother. She never received a reply.

Lena was aware of Annie Steele's existence, but had never met her. When *The Wiz* was being filmed in Astoria, Queens, Steele had attempted to see Lena but had been barred by an assistant. On opening night of *Lena Horne: The Lady and Her Music*, she had arrived at the door of the Nederlander Theater and, posing as Lena's daughter, Gail, managed to get the telephone number of

Lena's dressing room. Lena had answered and thought the voice that said, "Mom! How are you?" was Gail's. When Steele had identified herself, Lena had been dumbstruck, and Ralph Harris had grabbed the receiver and shouted, "Who gave you this number? Why are you doing this?"

Steele persisted. She got a friend, a commercial artist and public relations man, to call Sherman Sneed and persuade him to give her an appointment. Sneed listened to her story and said it was preposterous. Lena had never been to Alabama until she had visited the state under the auspices of the National Council of Negro Women in the 1960s. She had never lived in Berkeley, and in fact was in Europe at the time Steele placed her there. And, most important, Lena Horne knew she'd only had one daughter. Males might not know it when they father a child, but females don't have that particular problem.

Reader reaction to the article in the *Amsterdam News* showed strong opposition to the decision the editor had made when he ran the article. The paper's switchboard and mailroom were deluged, and a hastily convened delegation that included representatives from the NCNW, 100 Black Women, the New York State Commission on the Affairs of Women, the Urban League, the NAACP, and Delta visited the offices of the newspaper to register their shock and disapproval. Jean Noble, president of Delta and Lena's friend for some twenty years, was quoted in the next edition of the weekly: "If this woman had read Lena's books, she would have known that her story was coming from the weirdest of places. I'm shocked, too, at this kind of investigative reporting. . . . If there is anybody whose life is an open book, it's Lena. . . . Why would one suggest that Lena bore a child and then denied her? Nothing in her whole history could suggest such a thing. Don't you think she would have taken care of the child and acknowledged it as her own? Lena Horne could never plausibly be besmirched as someone who would desert a child."

Lena herself made no public statement about the Steele matter. She wouldn't lend it that much credence. Annie Steele was indeed unfortunate not to know the identities of her mother and father,

205

but Lena was not about to be used as a publicity vehicle. Steele was intent on "resuming her career." She'd told the *Amsterdam News*, "I sing classics and jazz. And I dance very well . . . I'm not out to hurt my mother in any way. I just want to get a successful job and get on with my career."

Several years earlier, a young man in Las Vegas had gone around to various clubs telling people he was Teddy, until he'd made the mistake of telling Billy Eckstine, an old and close friend of Lena's. When Eckstine told him off, the young man had just shrugged and said, "Oh well, I got some publicity."

Nearly two months before Annie Steele had received her publicity, Lena had announced that she would close on Broadway at last on June 30, 1982, her sixty-fifth birthday. The show's run had been extended four times and she had been forced to postpone commitments to take it elsewhere each time she had agreed to a further extension in New York. Her commitments to take the show to other cities had increased in the interim. Originally scheduled to perform in six cities before going to London, she now had committed herself to playing eight, and perhaps more. Once a firm closing date had been announced, tickets to the show were at a premium in the remaining weeks, and seats to the final performance were sold out by the end of March.

It was an emotion-filled farewell performance. Lena hadn't lost her sense of gratification at the way her "home town" had taken her in; she was also aware that she might not have the opportunity to appear on Broadway again. But she knew she had left her mark there, both literally and figuratively. The street sign at Forty-First Street and Seventh Avenue would henceforth read "Lena Horne Street," and *Lena Horne: The Lady and Her Music*, which had scored a record 333 mostly sold-out performances, was not only the longest-running one-woman show in the history of Broadway but the standard against which every future one-person show would be measured.

At her sixty-fifth birthday party at Roseland Ballroom afterward, eight hundred well-wishers cheered her entrance. Pinkerton guards tried to keep her in a fenced-off area, but she wouldn't have it. "I want to be with the people," she said as she marched into the crowd. During the evening, Seagram's Distillers, which had sponsored the party along with the show's producers, announced the establishment of an annual scholarship in her name at the Duke Ellington School of the Arts in Washington, DC.

Lena took no vacation after she closed on Broadway. She set out immediately on tour. On July 4-5 she was at Tanglewood in the Massachusetts Berkshires; on July 18-22 at Pine Knob outside Detroit; on July 25-26 at Wolf Trap outside Washington, DC; on July 30-August 1 at Poplar Creek outside Chicago; on August 17-22 at the Performing Arts Center in Denver; and on August 31-September 6 in Seattle.

In each of these places, Lena received the same kind of reception she had in New York. The audience was absolutely with her from the moment she walked onto the stage, and no doubt it occurred to her that much had changed in the life of a black touring performer over the years. Not only could she be exactly whom she wanted to be, but audiences applauded her for it.

That atmosphere changed, however, when she reached California where she played, for the first time on her tour, at theaters that maintained a subscription policy. In San Francisco, a city she loved, the audiences gave her a standing ovation at the end, but they didn't *participate* in the show the way audiences elsewhere had. Only at the preview performances were they really with her, and these crowds contained a mix of ages and races and geographical roots that did not obtain when the show opened to the subscription audience. Lena analyzed the subscription audience for a reporter from the *Los Angeles Herald-Examiner*: "They bought those tickets so they could see *Showboat* and *Colette*. Those people tend to be from the outskirts." The subscription audiences included very few blacks: "They resent having to sign a subscription to see plays they don't want to see just to see an entertainer they might like. And when the blacks do come, they have to sit on the aisles or upstairs because the subscription holders get the center seats."

By the time she was midway through her engagement in San Francisco, Lena learned that trouble was brewing over supposed discriminatory seating policies for her premiere show in Dallas, where she was scheduled to appear on January 18, two weeks after she closed in Los Angeles. Her premiere show at the Majestic Theatre, which would mark the reopening of the one-time vaudeville theater that had been purchased and renovated as an arts center by the city of Dallas, was supposed to be a benefit for Action for Cultural Arts, an organization that promotes arts in the city. Tickets for the opening gala were priced at $50-$600, and as soon as the prices were announced a city councilwoman named Elsie Fay Heggens had charged that they were a form of de facto discrimination against blacks. Lena, informed of the controversy, had the matter looked into, and the report she received caused her to cancel her Dallas engagement. In her official statement she said:

I have had a history of being involved in controversies where words like "racism" and "discrimination" were used. Yes, I want to cancel this engagement, but not for the reasons anyone has stated up to this point. I don't run away from controversy. I try to get the facts and then make a rational decision, one that is not based on fear of one side of the controversy or the other.

When I heard Heggens' statement I asked my manager to contact the local black organizations. We were told that none of them had been invited to the gala opening. We found that blacks in multi-racial organizations had been invited, but only a select few.

More important, and the reason I cannot blindly support the councilwoman's accusations, is that neither she nor the theater asked me how I felt about the issue at hand or informed me of what the true facts were. This was to have been a charitable event. Charity is something which should be supported by people who can afford it in the name of true charity, regardless of their color. Heggens used my name to draw national attention to a local issue, and I was made a pawn of some local politicians.

I do not want to be caught in the middle of a local dispute and used as a pawn or a symbol by either side. At this time, I must cancel the engagement.

From San Francisco, Lena went on to Los Angeles and the Pantages Theater, which also had a subscription policy. Again, there were few blacks, and comparatively few young people to visit her backstage and tell her that their parents or grandparents had told them about her but they had not really known what their elders were talking about until they had seen her themselves. She missed the audience "mix" with whom she communicated best and wasn't at all unhappy to have a few days off during the time that she was scheduled to have appeared in Dallas. But she recouped quickly, and she played four more cities before arriving in early May in Washington, DC, for a three-week run.

In the nation's capital, Lena became involved in another controversy. She learned that the Vista Hotel, where she was to appear at a fundraising reception for the NCNW, did not employ union workers and, being a very staunch supporter of unions, she insisted that the site of the reception be changed to the Shoreham Hotel, which was unionized. After she had made that announcement, she learned that the hotel where she was staying, the Four Seasons, also wasn't unionized. She arrived back at the hotel so late at night after her show that she hadn't seen the picket lines. She promptly moved from the Four Seasons to the Sheraton and on her arrival found her room looking like a florist's shop, filled with bouquets from the International Hotel Workers Union, the International Union of Operators, the Food and Beverage Trade Union and the Hotel and Restaurant Employees Union, not to mention the United Mine Workers Union, which had no direct connection with the controversy but had decided to thank her for her support of unionism in general.

From Washington, DC, Lena returned to New York to cohost the annual Tony awards presentation with Richard Burton and Jack Lemmon. She *still* hadn't gotten her show to London.

14

LENA, SENIOR CITIZEN

ONE of the few things about which Lena's opinions hadn't changed over the years was unions; she supported them now as adamantly as she had when she first arrived in Los Angeles, or when she had refused to perform on the ship that brought her and Lennie back from France after their secret marriage in 1947. In that sense, she had a tradition of supporting the cause of the "common man," no matter what his race, and no matter that a lot of white common men over the years hadn't done the same for her. Since the sixties, she'd come to realize that unions were even more central to the divisions between Americans than race, and that if a single, overriding issue could be identified, it would be economics. What divided people, and kept blacks down, was "an economic hype that has been laid on us since slavery time."

"I'm happy that IBM, AT&T and all those big combines are hiring more blacks than they ever did, but I still see a lot of poor people around," she told a reporter for *Women's Wear Daily* in 1981. "I see the whites as well as the blacks. I share the anger now with a lot of people. It's different than when it used to be just 'us, us.'"

She had observed that even the concern over relationships between black men and women, about which she had written and often spoken in the 1960s, seemed not to apply in cases where the couple had enough money and to apply equally to white couples who were in financial straits. "I think if both members of the wedding have a job, then it's okay," she told Gil Noble, "but money is going to keep us fighting each other and we blame it on race, but it doesn't have too much to do with that."

What disturbed her sometimes was her observation that young black people were concerned with little but money. She remembered a time when making money was secondary to pursuing one's principles. She acknowledged that the world had changed and envied the generation that had grown up not knowing the hardships of being black that she'd known, but she didn't envy the young people whose hardheaded view that money was the only "principle" worth working for blinded them to the wealth of feeling that she had known in the sixties and regretted not having experienced long before then. "Maybe what I miss from them is some sort of trying or hurting," she told Gil Noble. "I know they hurt, but the pain I'm talking about is the kind you feel when you see each other done in. That kind of pain, I find, is missing. . . . I see it in whites as well as blacks. I hear it's that way all over the world. I know in France and England they're cold, cold. There's a lack of any kind of warmth . . . I don't know why. Is it some change in molecular structure we've gone through and don't know it? Is it some genetic violence we've swallowed?"

Perhaps she was forgetting that she, too, had once lacked warmth and that it had had nothing whatsoever to do with genes. Her aloofness had been a response to her environment—first her family environment, or lack thereof, and then her societal environment. On the other hand, perhaps she was not forgetting her own personal history at all but only wishing that others wouldn't have to take as long as she had to find themselves.

She'd been emotionally transformed in the sixties, had virtually offered her former cold self on the pyre of the civil rights movement. She had identified with the pain of her people and allowed herself to feel that she was part of them in ways that she had either been ignorant of or denied before. And after a period of headlong feeling and resentment, she had effectively purged herself of the terrible coldness that had begun to settle into her soul when she was a child. Still, for a time she had merely substituted anger for aloofness and had come no closer to wisdom than she'd been before. It had taken the triple tragedy of the deaths of the three most important men in her life to crack her heart open and lay her feelings bare, to force her into the realization that she could work effectively for no person or cause unless she worked first for herself.

Only after she had lost the people whom she wanted to please and watched the movement for which she had wanted to be a success grind to a halt did she begin to enjoy performing. Having lost most of the people who had been closest to her, she was freed to regard her audiences as human beings, to let down the barriers she had erected to separate herself psychologically from them. They were no longer her adversaries, and she no longer had to appear before them in an attitude of total control. Once she began to welcome them, they in turn began to respond to her with a warmth that she had never before experienced.

Her singing changed. Even the songs that had long been associated with her took on more depth—her presentation was not merely a series of relatively clinical exercises in lyrical variation. Dalili Davis recalls that until the deaths of Lena's father, son, and husband, Lena's singing hadn't appealed to her. "But after the deaths of these men that she loved so dearly, her music got phenomenal. She started to remind me of Billie Holiday in the kind of depth that was coming out of her source, and I started being a Lena fan." But the change in her singing was also due to the change in her attitude toward her audiences. In fact, in the decade following the deaths she did an about-face in her comparative abilities to relate to individuals and groups: whereas before she had been most comfortable relating to others one-on-one, she found that she became more comfortable with audiences than with individuals.

She still needed to be with her family and still used the most tenuous blood and friendship connections to claim "family ties"; but she didn't want to cling. Her grandchildren were all teenagers by now, busy with their own lives; she joked that to see them she had to make an appointment. Gail, too, had her own life to pursue and was working on a book about the line of strong women from whom she was descended. Lena did not want her life to depend on family. Although she relied on individuals like Ralph Harris and Sherman Sneed, they had become inextricably a part of her life and career at the same time as her life and career had become closely bound up together. "Maybe I'm enjoying the career because there's nothing left but the career," she told Paul Rosenfield of the *Los Angeles Times* in 1982.

Other than the few individuals she cared about who were left, there was indeed no one but the audiences for Lena. She believed that it was the audiences who would determine how long she would be able to pursue her career.

The audiences . . . and time. On reaching the age of sixty-five, Lena had joked that she was pleased to be able to collect her Social Security and to ride public transportation and buy theater tickets at a discount. But like others who turn sixty-five, she faced the frightening realization that this chronological point in life not only signals that one has rounded the last bend in the road but also presents a stretch whose end is enveloped in mist. Just how long will it be, and when will it end? Not knowing wreaks havoc with plans for the future.

How long will the money last; how long will you have to make it last? By today's standards for stars, Lena Horne is not a particularly wealthy woman. She and Lennie shared a similar attitude about money in that they refused to work just for the sake of it. In fact they deliberately refused lucrative offers if they weren't interested in or believed they'd be uncomfortable in a job. They had indulged their love of travel but otherwise lived quite simply. They had hired only the best musicians to travel with them on the road, at the expense of greater profit. Lena had canceled engagements on principle, even though cancellation involved losing money, or having to pay out money, as happened when she refused to perform in Boston with Tony Bennett when that city was torn with racial strife over busing. Over the years she had also paid out a lot of money to take care of various family members. Continuing to work now, although not essential to her material comfort, wouldn't hurt her bank account and security, particularly when she had no idea how far that bank account would have to stretch.

Time would also have something to say about her looks, which she was pleased to have retained even though audiences had begun to come to hear her as well as see her. She realized that looking so much younger than she actually was had become part of her legend; in fact, it had raised her to a plane that, to some people, seemed slightly supernatural. In its review of her show on Broadway, *Time* magazine had referred to her "feral smile," and indeed there is something wild about her visage on the cover of the album sound track of the show. But is it "feral"? Might it not be read also as wildly triumphant rather than bestial? Was the *Time* correspondent unconsciously recalling some werewolf lore according to which humans who turn into wild beasts by night do not age? What if her beautiful, youthful face suddenly disintegrated, as in one of those B sci-fi movies? Would she still be celebrated for her singing alone, or would people go to see her primarily to cluck and shake their heads over what had happened to her beauty?

Lena was more concerned about her physical stamina, although she had found that a regimen of nightly excitement and standing ovations from audiences was as energizing as the vitamins she tried to remember to take every day. She wished that she was fifty again—not twenty or thirty or forty, but fifty—because it had been then that she really came into her own and realized that she could "go anywhere she wanted to." Time had quickened; she was in a hurry now. As she told Marcia Gillespie of *Ms.*:

> Psychologically something's pushing, pushing, pushing me. I seem to have this desire, this push, to get it all neat and together. I'm aware of time, that's all. I suppose that's natural at my age, but there's a sense of urgency about it. And I'm very frightened. You know, it's as if I never did anything before. I just don't want to stop without being where all the smarties, and the people who put the test to you, say it all is.

One suspects that this is not the first time Lena Horne has felt this way. In fact, there in her own words may be the real prescription for the almost legendary youthfulness and vitality of Lena Horne: Life, for her, has never ceased to be a thrilling adventure.

INDEX